St. Martín de Porres

FAITH AND CULTURES SERIES

An Orbis Series on Contextualizing Gospel and Church
General Editor: Robert J. Schreiter, C.PP.S.

The *Faith and Cultures Series* deals with questions that arise as Christian faith attempts to respond to its new global reality. For centuries Christianity and the church were identified with European cultures. Although the roots of Christian tradition lie deep in Semitic cultures and Africa, and although Asian influences on it are well documented, that original diversity was widely forgotten as the church took shape in the West.

Today, as the churches of the Americas, Asia, and Africa take their place alongside older churches of Mediterranean and North Atlantic cultures, they claim the right to express Christian faith in their own idioms, thought patterns, and cultures. To provide a forum for better understanding this process, the Orbis *Faith and Cultures Series* publishes books that illuminate the range of questions that arise from this global challenge.

Orbis and the *Faith and Cultures Series* General Editor invite the submission of manuscripts on relevant topics.

Also in the Series

Faces of Jesus in Africa, Robert J. Schreiter, C.PP.S., Editor
Hispanic Devotional Piety, C. Gilbert Romero
African Theology in Its Social Context, Bénézet Bujo
Models of Contextual Theology, Stephen B. Bevans, S.V.D
Asian Faces of Jesus, R. S. Sugirtharajah, Editor
Evangelizing the Culture of Modernity, Hervé Carrier, S.J.

FAITH AND CULTURES SERIES

St. Martín de Porres

The "Little Stories" and the Semiotics of Culture

Alex García-Rivera

ORBIS BOOKS
Maryknoll, New York 10545

The Catholic Foreign Mission Society of America (Maryknoll) recruits and trains people for overseas missionary service. Through Orbis Books, Maryknoll aims to foster the international dialogue that is essential to mission. The books published, however, reflect the opinions of their authors and are not meant to represent the official position of the society.

Library of Congress Cataloging in Publication Data

García-Rivera, Alex.
    St. Martín de Porres : the "little stories" and the semiotics of culture / Alex García-Rivera.
        p. cm. — (Faith and cultures series)
    Includes index.
    ISBN 1-57075-033-5 (alk. paper)
    1. Martín, de Porres, Saint, 1579-1639. 2. Christianity and culture. 3. Catholic Church—Latin America. 4. Mestizaje. 5. Latin America—Religious life and customs. I. Title. II. Series.
BX4700.M4218G37   1995
282′ .092—dc20   95-17445
                                      CIP

The wolf shall live with the lamb,
The leopard shall lie down with the kid,
the calf and the lion and the fatling together,
and a little child shall lead them.

Isaiah 11:6

Contents

Acknowledgments

This work properly belongs to the people of St. Martín de Porres Lutheran Church in Allentown, Pennsylvania, and the people of St. Leander's Roman Catholic Parish in San Leandro, California. Their devotion to St. Martín de Porres crosses boundaries that 500 years of official conflict have not been able to cross. Moreover, their faith, hope and charity instructed me in the power of the religious imagination and the profound wisdom of the poor. This work began under their tutoring and now, finished, I dedicate it primarily to them. Yet the completion of this work owes a great deal to my friend, Dr. Philip Hefner, who encouraged me to write my dissertation on St. Martín de Porres. If it had not been for his openness to the material and, indeed, his courage and skill in helping me follow the twisting paths of the creative act, my dissertation on St. Martín and, thus, this work would not have been written. I also owe a great intellectual debt to my friend, Dr. Virgilio Elizondo, whose works inspired me. I would not have walked into the area of popular religiosity if Dr. Elizondo had not opened the door. Having walked into that room, however, I would have been completely lost if it had not been for my mentor and dear friend, Dr. Robert Schreiter, who taught me the semiotics of culture and corrected my Latin at the same time. Dr. Schreiter gave me the tools by which to explore the world Dr. Elizondo had opened. I owe more to him than I can express. I also must express gratitude for the deep friendship and wise advice that Dr. Jose David Rodriguez shared with me. Dr. Rodriguez' friendship, coupled with his great insights into Latin American theology, made the writing of this work a sacramental experience. I would also like to thank the faculty and staff of the Jesuit School of Theology at Berkeley for welcoming me as one of their own and providing an atmosphere of intellectual excellence and spiritual warmth. I am especially grateful to Dean Dave Stagaman, SJ, who took a chance on me and to Mary Ann Donovan, SC, who introduced me to the intricacies of Pseudo-Dionysius. Finally, I owe more than I can say to Kathryn, my wife and best friend, and my children, Sophia and Elisabet, who supported me emotionally (and Kathryn with the editing) during this arduous process. Indeed, this work was written by a community and to all of you, I offer my deepest thanks and friendship.

Unless otherwise noted, all materials that are cited in editions in languages other than English have been translated by me.

Foreword

Virgil Elizondo

The best way to introduce this fascinating breakthrough in contemporary theological writings is to introduce the author. Such an original work could only come from the creative imagination and critical intellect of a very unique human being such as Alex García-Rivera. He is, first of all, a very ordinary human being who is very much in love with his wife and family and struggles daily to be a good husband and good father. Alex loves being a simple human being, but he is no ordinary human being!

Alex is a Cuban exile who has lived the painful experience of a foreigner struggling for identity, acceptance, and belonging. He is a physicist turned Lutheran pastor who discovered St. Martín de Porres while working with the Hispanic poor of Pennsylvania. His fascination with the world of science, coupled with his love and pastoral concern for the people he was called to serve, led him to pursue further studies to become better equipped to minister properly to his people. St. Martín de Porres, however, was not yet finished with Alex. In coming to know St. Martín de Porres in his graduate studies, Alex discovered his own religious roots and eventually returned to his original Roman Catholicism.

I first met Alex just before he started graduate studies in theology. During one of my courses, he became fascinated with the evangelical possibilities of *Mestizaje* and the role Our Lady of Guadalupe played in the birth, formation, and development of the Mexican and Mexican-American consciousness. Alex saw much more in what I was teaching than I had imagined myself! We had many fascinating and challenging conversations over the interrelationships among science, faith, and theology. We quickly became brothers in the common search for the ultimate meaning and mission of our Latino mestizo ethnicity within the U.S., and we continue to enjoy each other's friendship and learn much from each other.

As Alex continued his doctoral studies at the Lutheran School of Theology in Chicago, he became so well versed in the classical European theologians that he could teach them in any classroom. The excellent and demanding guidance of professors Philip Hefner, Robert Schreiter, and Jose David Rodriguez led him not simply to write about others, but to give birth to his own thought based on the popular devotion to San Martín de Porres. In the beginning, no one thought this was a proper topic for a doctoral dissertation, but Alex was persistent and gradually made converts of everyone.

Through a careful, critical, and creative study of the collective memory of this Peruvian mulatto, Alex was able to discern, formulate, and organize a new understanding of the universal meaning and potential of *Mestizaje*. From a very particular and well-defined study of one person, he has been able to develop a theory that is universally applicable and urgently needed in today's world of growing ethnic divisions. Alex elaborates very original theological and anthropological theories that, I have no doubt, will stir up much serious and creative discussion.

Because he dares to be so particular and well defined, Alex is a universal theologian. He is a new theologian because as a man of faith he challenges the physical and social sciences in furthering the understanding of the human condition. He is a critical theologian because there is no doubt about the depth and seriousness of his work. He is a devotional theologian because he develops new theological breakthroughs based on the devotional life of the people. He is a pastoral theologian because his work has immediate implications in the lives and ministry of the people.

I have no doubt that this book will stand as a landmark in new theological developments. It is easy to read and fascinating to explore. It is about San Martín de Porres, but it is really about the radicalness of Christian living in the midst of very un-Christian circumstances. Even more so, it is about a new image of the human that much of the rational, critical, and technological world does not suspect. In the world that dehumanized the poor and unwanted of society, St. Martín, himself a despised mulatto, gave all of us a new understanding of what it means to be truly human and truly Christian.

As one of the first American saints, San Martín stands as a vision of hope that a truly new America might come to be. He is among the firstborn of the new Creation of the Americas. He offers us a new vision—not with his theories and writings, but with the witness of his life. Alex has done a great service in presenting Martín de Porres as the model of the new human being of the Americas.

Introduction

Robert J. Schreiter

Alex García-Rivera's reading of the "little stories" of St. Martín de Porres is a signal event in the development both of a new method and a new discourse in theology. He brings together for the first time a variety of perspectives and methods, refines them, and uses them to open up to us a discourse that is at once revelatory of another world and a mirror for our own. He does this not only with careful analytic skill, but also with the keen awareness of what happens to people in the violent and unequal encounter of cultures. For the world of this encounter is his world, which puts him in a special position to bring the "little stories" to bear on the "big stories" of established theology.

In order to appreciate the significance of what García-Rivera proposes, it might be useful to highlight five elements that he brings to bear on the stories of St. Martín. To dwell on these five elements both introduces his work and situates it within larger discussions about reading such stories now going on within theology and literature and about culture in general. These in turn point further to the potential they have for transforming how we engage in theology, how it grows from the underside of history, and how it might be linked to other theological discourses.

The first element is García-Rivera's extension of the concept of *mestizaje*. This concept is about the mixing of peoples and cultures in the violent and unequal encounter of the *Conquista* and the consequences of that mixing. This concept had developed in Latin American philosophy and literature in the nineteenth and twentieth centuries, but it was Virgil Elizondo who has made it central to Hispanic and Latino theologies. Seeing in *mestizaje* the imprint of Jesus of Nazareth's Galilean identity and ministry, Elizondo has helped theologians and others see that such mixing is not a mongrelization of humanity, but an enrichment of it and a potential source of grace as well. García-Rivera helps make more explicit some of Elizondo's insight by showing its dynamics in the St. Martín stories. In so doing, he demonstrates his assertion that *mestizaje* is not merely the mixing of cultures with the peoples implicated as passive objects of the violent and unequal encounter. To be sure, the conquerors' power *is* beyond their control. But within those powerful encounters, even conquered people do not lose their power to act and to form their worlds. The examples that jump out in the St. Martín stories underscore that more than any dogmatic assertion.

By thus extending our concept of *mestizaje,* García-Rivera is making a contribution to the wider discussion of how to understand culture, both in these historical contexts, but also today. In contemporary postcolonial writing, formerly subjugated peoples are trying to reconstruct their identities, not simply by imagining a precolonial past, but by coming to terms with the many strands of culture in which they participate. With the unprecedented migration of peoples around the planet, as well as the impact of global communication technologies and circulation of cultural images in music and video, nearly everyone everywhere is part of a great cultural churning. This creolization or hybridization of cultures undercuts long-held assumptions about cultures being relatively enclosed, integrated wholes. García-Rivera adds to that discussion with his expanded concept of *mestizaje,* especially to the role of human agency as it encounters the power of the conqueror.

A second element worth highlighting here is his reading of the St. Martín texts. Antonio Gramsci's proposals for a subaltern or under-side reading of struggle have been known since the publications of parts of his prison notebooks. His basic point—that subjugated peoples do not simply accept the world imposed upon them but fashion one of their own, often unbeknownst to the hegemonic power over them—has reached a good measure of acceptance in many circles. A continuing problem has been developing a method that opens up that subaltern world in a way respectful of that world: not just the symmetrical mirror-image of the hegemonic world, nor the hoped-for conclusions of the investigator. Some attempts to discover the subaltern world by outsiders can look suspiciously close to projection. Often the results are far too neat and tidy, which belies the violence that keeps hegemony in place. By an adept use of semiotic method, García-Rivera provides a way into the subaltern world, showing how codes and signs are reversed. The reader will no doubt delight in the ironies and reversals that can be discovered when the lay brother heals the Bishop of México, when aristocratic courts are compared to latrines (and lose in the comparison!), when the mulatto heals the "pure." Recent years have witnessed a number of subaltern readings of the violent and unequal encounter of cultures in the Americas, especially since the quincentennial commemoration of that event. The readings of the little stories of St. Martín contribute to that literature with an incision and clarity not always seen.

It is García-Rivera's insightful development of semiotics as a tool for understanding culture and theology that is the third important element to be highlighted here. He may found the beginning of his study of semiotics in my own work, but he has carried it forward substantially, particularly through his reading of subsequent work of Juri Lotman and C.S. Peirce. Specifically, he makes three contributions. The first is his concept of the mosaic as a way of imagining the interplay of signs. Just as the pieces of mosaic can be positioned differently, and their possible relations to one another might constitute a variety of patterns or messages, so too juxtapositions of signs allow cultures to communicate (and to conceal) in different ways. Thinking through the proposal of the mosaic will help us understand the *mestizaje* being undergone today.

Closely allied with that is his second contribution, namely, his understanding of the dynamics of the boundary and the boundary's potential to create new semiotic domains. Much is made of this in poststructuralist and postcolonialist writing, but García-Rivera takes us beyond assertion to demonstrate how this takes place. His examination of the ladder and the animal-human boundary in the little stories exemplify this especially. Margins and boundaries can be powerful places as well as alienating ones. García-Rivera has given us a way to understand them better. Thus, for theology, when we speak of God dwelling on the boundaries, we get a clearer picture of why God might do that and what that means.

His third contribution addresses an objection frequently raised regarding semiotics: that its readings are synchronic, and cannot take into account history. By his reading of the animal signs (especially "dog"), García-Rivera hopes to give a history to the sign. At first glance this might not appear to be the case, for who knows if the interlocutors in the story knew those histories? But to require such is to impose one theory of reading and one set of cultural assumptions on the text—that all potential meaning must be in the mind of the speaker/author, and that uneducated people have no history. García-Rivera's carefully laid framework undercuts such objections. His reading of the text is not bound by the Romanticist assumption that the author only may make the text. Semiotic reading itself more or less assumes that the author is part of a larger semiotic or sign-making process. That oral peoples have no history, do not have historical memory, is a common bias of literate peoples. What García-Rivera reveals here, therefore, is that signs *do* have a history. And that is probably especially the case for the peoples on the underside, who must artfully conceal their histories from the conquerors who would like to believe that they have remade them.

All in all, our understanding and use of semiotic method has been advanced by this work. What García-Rivera has done stands apart from the semiotic work being done in theology in Germany, France, and the Netherlands today. It will be interesting to see, over the long run, what influences these methods will have on his, as well as his on theirs. In any event, for reading little stories in the often violent mixing of cultures today—the experience of many, if not most Christians—the tools presented here will be of immense use.

García-Rivera's background in the physical sciences contributes the fourth element worth noting here: that is his concept of *asymmetry*. Asymmetry already figures largely in deconstructionist readings of texts, but largely as a destabilizing factor that ultimately dissolves the sign. Symmetric relations, on the other hand, are understood almost exclusively from the standpoint of power: hegemony masked as harmony. García-Rivera is well aware of all of this, but by introducing a more capacious understanding of asymmetry, he is able to unlock its transformational power. To be sure, symmetry as an aesthetic concept can mask the strains of domination, making some forms of hierarchy appear "natural," even graceful. But as his analysis of the Valladolid debates and the boundaries between human and animal indicates, asymmetry not only topples absurd and unjust orderings of people and things, it also generates new possibilities, new ways of imagining relationships in the world. García-Rivera's understanding of asymmetry is suffused with a generosity and a hospitality that is life-giving, even in the midst of the struggle. It is reflected already earlier in the book in his discussion of the relation of the little stories to the big stories; the little stories can call the big stories' versions of events into profound question, but at the same time leave room for new possibilities. It is that generosity and hospitality that allow the poor to survive and to celebrate in the midst of protracted struggle without succumbing to cynicism and bitterness.

That appreciation of the generosity as well as the destabilizing potential of asymmetry leads to the final point to be highlighted here. This appears in his reflections at the end of the book on theological anthropology, the understanding of the human. He refers to it as "a horizontal fellowship of sacramental grace." In the powerful image of the dog, the cat and the mouse sharing human food, a new vision of relationship within the world is imagined. The semiotic domain of the "human" is redrawn. What he proposes here is an anthropology that does not define itself exclusively as an anthropology of resistance—although without resistance it cannot survive and runs the risk of losing its humanity—but a more ample anthropology, one not defined solely by its resistance to oppression. It is an anthropology informed by a sacramental grace that García-Rivera elaborates in Eucharistic terms. It is a place where all commune together. In a time when communities and theologies have had to define themselves in terms of resistance and now must struggle with the ambiguities of participating in the reconstruction of communities and societies, the theological anthropology represented in St. Martín's little stories offers a way of imagining the future. García-Rivera, in this little book of little stories, has helped bring us to that. Not only do we see more clearly the message of St. Martín for our own day and time, he has given us tools for examining that day and time that needs the grace and the graciousness of this gentle figure.

García-Rivera closes the book by urging us to engage our imagination—

no doubt hinting at where his own thinking is developing. We can only eagerly anticipate where that might lead. This is the first book of a creative and engaging mind. We all can only be grateful that he is putting such gifts to the task of understanding how faith and culture might meet.

1

A Mystery in Lima

All human beings are essentially the same. Or are they? The Old World believed human beings were distinguished from the animals by their reason. Reason was the universal principle that bound human beings in fellowship. This assumption was challenged at Lima. New questions were asked and new answers given. Are there true differences between human beings? If so, on what basis can there be true human fellowship? The mystery lies in that this important debate did not take place in the halls of a university but, rather, in the beatification process of the mulatto saint, Martín de Porres. At issue was the very meaning of human being.

The theological debate over human being that took place in the beatification process of St. Martín de Porres took the form of a series of eyewitness stories. What is surprising is that these stories differ from the stories told at colleges and universities. These institutions concentrate on the "Big Story." The "Big Story" tells a story of universal principles believed to be responsible for human being, giving it locus and meaning in the cosmos. For example, the great theologian Karl Rahner tells us that "man is the infinity of absolute spiritual openness for being" (Rahner 1981, 24). This is a "Big Story." Yet who can understand it?

Actually, a few can. Scholars and theologians make up a select group of individuals who have been trained in the art of disclosing the universals of human being and its place in the cosmos. There is nothing wrong with such a specialized group (Sullivan 1988). Their contributions are essential to any society. Nonetheless, in recent centuries, the "Big Story" they tell is increasingly understood only by other members of the same specialized group. More often than not, the "Big Story" account of reality turns out to be not so much a universal tale of human being, but merely a skewed or specialized story, an insider's story that makes sense only to those who tell it. Such a complaint is more than a call for clarity or a recall of technical language. More is at stake. A "Big Story," as a true and universal account of human reality, affects all members of society. Such a story has more than understanding as a goal for its telling. Such a story discloses the paths of life we are to follow. The question to be asked of Rahner's "Big Story" is not "what does it mean?" but, rather, "for whom is it for?"

There exists another type of story, the "little story" told outside the bounds of academia. "Little stories" are told by specialists and nonspecialists, by assembly line workers and university professors alike. They are not told to replace the "Big Story" but, instead, to make such a story possible. One such set of "little stories" concerns the Dominican mulatto saint, St. Martín de Porres.

Who was Martín de Porres? A contemporary who knew him, Fray Antonio Gutiérrez, describes him as (Secretariado Martín de Porres 1960):

> a man of great charity, who being in charge of the infirmary not only healed his brother religious when they were sick but also assisted in the larger duty of spreading the Great Love of the world. For this they knew him as their father and consolation, calling him father of the poor. Moreover, he cared for lay people outside [these walls] from every state of life, healing them of their pains, wounds, and inflammations and other hurts they had, bleeding and healing them through his own person and thus an infinite number sought him out and all found in him some help: the sick, relief; the afflicted, consolation; and the rest, refuge. He did this willingly, his semblance happy and peaceful. And after having shown such charity with these, his neighbors without exception, he would do the same with animals, and, in particular, with dogs, for having found them wounded or hurt in the streets, he would take them to his cell and healed them with the same care as if they were rational and he would give them to eat and take care of them until they were well at which point he would ask them to leave. And even with the mice, who, having damaged clothing used for the sick, he commanded them to a place which he pointed out and there he brought them whatever food they needed.[1]

St. Martín was an incredible man. What makes this assessment even more incredible is the fact that he was born a *casta* or *mulatto,* the son of the white, blue-eyed Spanish hidalgo[2] Don Juan de Porres[3] and the freed black slave Ana Velázquez.[4] Although Martín's parents met in Panama, he was born in Lima on December 9, 1575. The baptismal entry in the registry of the church of San Sebastian[5] simply reads: "On Wednesday, the ninth of November of 1579 I baptized Martín, son of an unknown father" (*Proceso,* 40).

Don Juan apparently did not wish to make public the fact of his mulatto son. In doing so, Don Juan condemned his son to illegitimacy, a serious consequence in the strictly hierarchical society of Lima. St. Martín could expect little support from his society. Thus it is even more incredible that St. Martín not only became loved by all in Lima but even gained back his father's name. The priest may not have put Martín's name on the register but Martín did not lose it. To this day, St. Martín is known as St. Martín de Porres.

Don Juan, however, did not shirk his obligation to see to Martín's education and provided him with an apprenticeship at the age of twelve to a barber, Dr. Marcelo de Ribera of Lima. In those days, a barber cut more than hair. They let out blood, treated wounds and fractures, and prescribed medicines. St. Martín learned the medical arts of the day through his apprenticeship with Dr. Ribera. His mother was well known for her knowledge of medicinal herbs and most probably taught him what she knew. St. Martín became quite famous for his healing. Francisco Pérez Quintero, master carpenter of the *Convento*, tells the following story:

> One time, while working at the *convento* in my capacity as carpenter I became sick with extreme cramps which put me to bed for three or four months. Dr. Navarro, an esteemed doctor from this city, tried several treatments but each time I got worse. The doctor then ordered that the Holy Sacraments be given to me and told me I would no doubt die . . . And one day while I remained in this condition said venerable fray Martín de Porras came into my cell with another religious brother, a companion of his, and they both picked me up and took me to the cell of said venerable fray Martín de Porras and made the bed for him and put him there. Then said venerable brother put two bricks, the hottest one he could find, one on his feet and another on the stomach, and covered him with many blankets and left, letting him rest. The witness slept from about nine in the morning until four in the afternoon when said venerable fray brother Martín de Porras came in to bring him something to eat. And he ate quite well and from then on, he continued the treatment and got better without any further medicine than that described and within a few days became healthy and well.[6]

St. Martín healed those the doctors of his day gave up for dead. No doubt, a creative synthesis of medical knowledge from his mother and the conventional medicine of his day gave him an edge.

At the age of sixteen, St. Martín presented himself as *donado* to the Dominican friars of the Convento del Santo Rosario. A donado was a member of the Third Order who, while living at the Convento, received food and lodging for the work he did as a lay helper (Preher 1941, 15). In Iberian eyes, this kind of work was menial and not fit for the lay brothers of the Convento. As a donado, Martín received a habit composed of a white tunic and a black cape. Don Juan, now Governor of Panama, was furious at St. Martín's inscription as a donado. It was a personal humiliation to himself that his son, even if unacknowledged as such, would spend the rest of his life in such menial labor.

When Don Juan attempted to get his son accepted into the Dominican Order itself, he was told that St. Martín had refused the offer several times. It is also true, however, that there existed laws against this.[7] The bishop in McBride's biography put it this way: "There are laws that we must respect. These indicate that the Indians, blacks and their descendants, cannot make profession in any religious order, seeing that they are races that have little formation as of yet" (McBride 1968, 16). Nonetheless, such laws could be broken. The prior of the Convento, Juan de Lorenzana, was more than willing to make St. Martín a regular lay brother, yet St. Martín refused. It was not until 1603, when he was twenty-four years old, that St. Martín made the profession of vows as a regular lay brother (Preher 1941, 16).

St. Martín lived out the rest of his days at the monastery. During his stay, he became known throughout Lima for his skill in healing; his social work among widows, orphans, and prostitutes; his founding of hospitals and orphanages; his work with the indigenous, black, mestizos, and mulatto poor of the city; and for his love of animals. St. Martín, in fact, was known as the "St. Francis of the Americas." In his lifetime, he was considered a miracle worker and became a popular saint even before his death.

St. Martín died on November 3, 1639, at the moment the choir at his deathbed chanted the *homo factus est* ("and was made human") of the Credo (Procurator General 1672, 117-9). The homo factus est points to the meaning of the following "little story" told by Fray Fernando Aragones:

> One of the Dominican friars in St. Martín's convent walked into a room near the kitchen to find a strange sight. At the feet of St. Martín were a dog and a cat eating peacefully from the same bowl of soup. The friar was about to call the rest of the monks in to witness this marvelous sight when a little mouse stuck his head out from a little hole in the wall. St. Martín without hesitation addressed the mouse as if he were an old friend. "Don't be afraid little one. If you're hungry come and eat with the others." The little mouse hesitated but then scampered to the bowl of soup from which the dog and the cat were eating. The friar who was watching all this take place tried to speak but no sound came out of his mouth. Here before his eyes, at the feet of the mulatto St. Martín, a dog, a cat, and a mouse were eating from the same bowl of soup, natural enemies eating peacefully side by side!

This "little story," like Rahner's "Big Story," also tells a story about the meaning of our humanity. Human beings are as different from one another as a dog is from a cat and a cat is from a mouse. These differences, however, do not necessarily make us natural enemies of one another. We are bound in common fellowship. Each of us is, after all, a *criatura de Dios,* a creature of

God. Our creatureliness becomes the basis for sharing our resources. We all can drink from the same bowl of soup, for we are creatures not of some universal humanity but of one Creator.

The "little story" of the dog, the cat, and the mouse may deceive the specialist of the academy or the Church. Its simplicity gives the impression such stories were meant for children. Yet if the Author of the "Big Story" is, as Leonard Bernstein's "Mass" celebrates, "the simplest of all," then the "little stories" are well suited to speak of the profundity of things.[8] The simple and the profound go together. The concern, then, is not to get rid of the specialist or of the art of disclosing the universal principles of human reality. The concern, rather, is to disclose the conditions that make such an art possible in the first place. These conditions are the existence of the "little stories" which are deceptively simple yet communicate essential information about the nature of our world and ourselves.

The "little stories" thus may be the antidote for the contemporary malaise affecting our society's specialists—the twin complaints of lack of meaning and irrelevance. The "little stories" promise the possibility of the return to the "Big Story," a return of meaning and relevance in our present social restlessness and lack of direction. Such is the case with the "little stories" of St. Martín de Porres. Hidden in the simplicity of the "little stories" of St. Martín de Porres is a "Big Story" about human being. The dog, cat, and mouse story, for example, reveals such a "Big Story," a "Big Story" that is revealed through the "little stories" told at Lima.

Lima was a natural place for "making saints." She produced five, all born in the same century: Santo Toribio Alfonso de Mongrevejo (1606), San Francisco Solano (1616), Santa Rosa de Lima (1617), Beato Juan Macías (1639) and, of course, St. Martín de Porres (1639) (Dussel 1987, 77; Clissold 1972, 61). But of all of these, only Martín was of mixed race. That a mulatto would even be considered as a candidate for canonization is surprising, yet St. Martín was known as a saint even before he died. Santa Rosa de Lima, daughter of an aristocratic white Spanish family in Lima, was canonized as saint by Pope Clement X in 1671. She had been baptized at the same baptismal font in the church of San Sebastian as had St. Martín, except that her baptism took place seven years later (Alphonsus 1968, 57). Martín was not canonized until May 6, 1962, by Pope John XXIII. As such, a mystery is involved. Why was St. Martín, loved by all, not canonized until this late date?

Some may cynically ask: What is the mystery? Such is to be expected from a racist Church. Such a condemnation is unfair and naïve. Fray Bartolomé del Rosario, a lay religious of Martín's Dominican Order, tells the following account of the day St. Martín's remains were exhumed:

> And on that day so many people came and gathered in the church, that there almost was no room for anyone. Furthermore, this witness did not nor gave orders to anyone to publicly announce the exhumation for

the desire was to be discreet, the exhumation taking place in as decent
a manner as required of a religious of the Order. Nonetheless, the
people who came included the Excsmo. Sr. Conde de San Esteban,
Virrey of these Kingdoms, the Lords of the Royal Audiencia, and other
superior tribunals. After them came the Cabildo, Justicias, and
Regimiento [i.e., the entire City Hall] of this city, and many religious
from many different Orders, captains of the Infantry and many gentle-
men, and other honorable persons of this Republic.

  Such a testimony challenges the cynical answer above. Members of all
races and power groups saw St. Martín as *their* saint. Moreover, the Church
did eventually beatify and canonize St. Martín. A purely racist attitude would
have dismissed St. Martín from the pages of Church history. And this is where
the mystery lies. What was it about St. Martín de Porres that transcended
social and cultural barriers—indeed, time? Cultural and racial prejudice
were, of course, involved in the time taken for Martín to be recognized by
the Church as one of her saints. Yet something more profound than racial
attitudes or social hierarchies was involved. That "something" was a deeper
human need, a search for a new "Big Story."
  The mystery at Lima involves a "Big Story" or rather the transformation
of a "Big Story." The fifteenth and sixteenth centuries were times of exploration and conquest from the perspective of Europe. The initiators of this
exploration were the inhabitants of the Iberian Peninsula: the Portuguese and
the Spanish. The Portuguese began this age of exploration and conquest by
sailing south along the coast of Africa. Although the continent of Africa had
been known since ancient times, that which lay beyond the Madeiras was
not. The Portuguese "discovery" of sub-Saharan Africa was a major feat of
European exploration. The Spanish sailed west. Through these explorations,
three continents collided in a violent and unequal encounter of cultures.[9]
  The greatest impact of this collision may have been a new understanding
of *difference*. As Todorov expressed it (1984, 4):

the discovery of America, or of the Americans, is certainly the most
astonishing encounter of our history. We do not have the same sense of
radical difference in the "discovery" of other continents and of other
peoples: Europeans have never been altogether ignorant of the existence of Africa, India, or China; some memory of these places was
always there already—from the beginning. The moon is farther away
than America or Europe, true enough, but today we know that our
encounter with it is no encounter at all, and that this discovery does not
occasion surprises of the same kind: for a living being to be photo-
graphed on the moon, an astronaut must stand in front of the camera,
and in his helmet we see only one reflection, that of another earthling.
At the beginning of the sixteenth century, the Indians of America are

certainly present, but nothing is known about them. . . . The encounter will never again achieve such intensity.

Europe had known difference,[10] but not with such intensity, such radicality. As Jonathan Z. Smith put it, "what a difference a 'difference' makes" (Smith 1985, 3-48), especially for Europe.

The notice of radical difference began with the first observations of the animals of America. Oviedo, for example, noticed that the big cats of America were not the same as the tigers of classical and medieval bestiaries.[11] This was close to heresy. In his *Etymologies,* Isidore of Seville (1911) had "mapped" the "little story" of Noah's ark to the known geography of the world—Europe, Asia, and Africa. The nations of Shem, Japhet, and Ham were mapped to Europe, Asia, and Africa, respectively. Moreover, all creatures that were carried in the ark were to be found in Europe, Asia, and Africa. What Isidore had created was a sacred geography, a cosmic "Big Story." This geography knew no other nations of people nor any new animal species. The encounter with the New World challenged Isidore's sacred geography through the presence of the Amerindian and the new species of animals in America. The New World had put the current version of Christian Europe's "Big Story" on notice.

Such challenges led Jonathan Z. Smith to conclude that the New World challenged the Old not simply on the basis that it was "merely 'new' or merely 'different.' " The challenge came (and still remains) as the reality of true difference, radical difference. The theoretical issues posed by the otherness of America, says Smith (1985, 44), were "raised in sharp form as a project of language." Words had yet to be found to describe the difference of America's people and animals. Yet it would be misleading to leave the impression that this "project of language" was only taken on by the Old World. Africa's and the New World's "Big Story" had also been challenged. There was, in effect, another project of language launched, a project to find a new "Big Story" by a new group in the Americas.

This new group consisted of a people caught between the Old World and the New, the new humanity born out of the violent and unequal encounter of cultures, the mestizos.[12] St. Martín was a member of this new group. A mestizo of Iberian and African blood, he was also profoundly influenced by contact with the indigenous culture of Lima.[13] Yet in a sense, all the inhabitants were mestizos. By 1600, a generation of Iberians had been born in Lima, their world shaped and formed by the marvelous mix of cultures. These people were known as *criollos.* Thus, all the mestizos of Lima—criollos, mulattos, and mestizos, but also peninsular Iberians who had assimilated the new reality of the Americas—were participating in a great movement toward self-understanding, a new world of meaning, a semiosis of a *novus mundus.*

The hearers of the "little stories" of St. Martín de Porres knew a "Big

Story" was in trouble. An alternative was proposed through the striking proposal that a mulatto of the New World be accepted among the saints of the Old World. The proposal came in the form of the "little stories" of the beatification process. This work is an attempt to "read" these "little stories" and articulate the alternative understanding of human being represented in the life and person of Martín de Porres.

2

Finding the "Little Story"

Where can the "little story" be found? The question is, in a sense, a fundamental question for Latin American theology. In the middle seventies, a group of Latin American Church historians attempted to write a history of the Church in Latin America that took into account Latin America's native genius. The group, headed by Enrique Dussel, was known formally as CEHILA (Commission for a Study of the History of the Church in Latin America). CEHILA aimed to publish a history of the Latin American Church that was researched and written by Latin Americans themselves. The members of CEHILA were convinced that the Latin American Church possessed its own authentic spirit.

But where could this spirit be found? Official documents and theological writings are traditional places to start. The native Latin American Church, however, left few written records, so the authentic Latin American Church had to be found in nontraditional records—in "symbols, poems, songs," or in "certain ecclesial or Christian practices," such as the "making" of saints, such as St. Martín de Porres (Richard 1980, 12). CEHILA's question was part of a larger question raging among the bishops and leaders of the Latin American Church. The question arose in the wake of Vatican II and was unique to the Latin American Church.

LATIN AMERICA AND POPULAR RELIGION

When most Roman Catholic (and Protestant) theologians are asked what they consider the most significant event of the sixteenth century, they point to the Reformation. The Roman Catholicism of Latin America, however, challenges this judgment. The Reformation and the conquest of America were contemporaneous events. The Latin American Church was influenced more by the conquest and evangelization of America than by the European struggle of the Reformation. Indeed, a distrust of the Latin American clergy by Europeans prevented Latin American Catholicism from being represented in any significant sense at the Council of Trent. As many cultural outsiders have observed, the Latin American Church (before Vatican II) resembled the Church of the fifteenth century more closely than the Tridentine Church after the Reformation.

The foundation of Latin American Catholicism took place not at the level of a struggle between official doctrines, as in Reformation Europe, but at the level of a struggle of popularizing the teachings of the Church to the newly baptized indigenous of America. In this endeavor, the friars began many new practices that combined ancient indigenous rituals and ancient Church tradition. This mixture of traditions continues to the present day, but not without suspicion. The Catholicism of Latin Americans has always been suspect. Its mixture of indigenous, African, and European elements makes it different from the Catholicism of Europe. Thus, the effect of Vatican II on the Latin American Church was not so much a reevaluation of the Tridentine Church as a reevaluation of the popular Church as described by the Bishops of Latin America.

In the vast baptized masses of Latin America, the conditions for faith, beliefs and practices are quite diverse, not only from one country to another, but also between regions within the same country, and between the various social levels. One finds semipagan ethnic groups; rural groups which maintain their profound religiosity and marginalized masses with religious sensibilities, but of low Christian practice. A process of cultural and religious transformation exists. The evangelization of the continent is experiencing various difficulties, which are aggravated by the demographic explosion, internal migrations, socio-cultural changes, the lack of apostolic personnel and a deficient adaptation by ecclesial structures.

The above description was voiced at the meeting of CELAM at Medellín, Colombia, in 1968. This was, of course, the meeting in which the Roman Catholic bishops came together to interpret Vatican II from a Latin American perspective. The meeting produced a series of documents that could be called the Magna Carta of liberation (Candelaria 1990, 19). Although best known for its documents on justice, peace, and poverty, Document VI, "Pastoral Popular," has become increasingly significant.

The "Pastoral Popular" recognized that post-Vatican II Latin America must find a sense of what popular religion means.[1] Such understanding, however, was hampered by two main attitudes to popular religion.[2] One attitude, the concern of the religious left, involved an elitist approach to pastoral practice. The Church, some claimed, was a heroic minority in battle with the fatalist tendencies of the popular, which co-opt the true message of liberation found in the gospels.[3] The other attitude, the concern of the religious right, involved a perceived syncretism of non-Christian symbols by popular religion. The Church, according to this group, ought to wage holy war against non-Christian symbols.

Such tension[4] reveals that something "Big" is at stake—the difference of the Latin American Church. It would seem that in the debate on the significance of popular religion, the issue of difference is still very much alive. If so, popular religion may be a fecund locus for theological reflection. Its manifestations may be symptoms of a "Big Story" in trouble or a new "Big Story" about to be born. A theologian who has taken the latter view is Virgilio Elizondo.

VIRGILIO ELIZONDO

A pastor and theologian, Elizondo is an Hispanic-American priest living in San Antonio, Texas. Elizondo could be considered a pioneer of the art of "little story" telling. His great contribution came as a positive, but convincing, evaluation of popular religion. This took considerable courage for Elizondo. His positive evaluation of popular religion made him a target of both the religious right and left. Elizondo's treatment of popular religion, however, went beyond their concerns. Elizondo wanted to understand the "little stories" of popular religion not as a sociologist or anthropologist but as a theologian. Historically, popular religion has been studied, in the main, by social scientists. Elizondo is one of the few theologians who found the possibility of a "Big Story" in popular religion. He proposed that the task of a theologian ought to be not the "canonization or rejection" of the religious symbols of a people but a "continuous re-interpretation" of them with respect to the gospel. Such reinterpretation, he was convinced, would lead people to the "Big Story," a "deeper knowledge of the saving God" (Elizondo 1977, 32).

His work is perhaps best described through his own "little stories." Elizondo (1988, x) describes his reality as living in a very special frontier:

I had always lived on the frontier between two worlds: Mexico and the United States. I had not chosen to live there and neither had I migrated there. In San Antonio I felt at home among my own. Yet all my life I had felt pulled in two opposing directions—the U.S. way of life and the Mexican way of life. Sometimes I felt the pull would be so great that it would rip me apart. But I could not run away either to the United States or to Mexico, for both were as much a part of me as I was a part of them.

Living in such a frontier presented Elizondo with a problem of identity. Was he Mexican or from the United States?

There were identities that I knew that I was and was not at the same time: U.S.-American, Mexican, Spanish, Indian. Yet I was! My very being was a combination. *I was a rich mixture but I was not mixed up!* At the same time, we had not yet pronounced a word that could name who we were. We were an emerging people whose identity had not yet been named. Of the new identity—neither this nor that but fully both—there was no doubt whatsoever. Yet the search for a name would dominate the quest of artists, intellectuals, social scientists, and poets for decades to come. And as of today we have not yet succeeded in finding the proper family name for this new human group on the planet earth. (Elizondo 1988, 27)

Elizondo, like millions of other frontier Texans, lived a dual life affirmed by neither culture yet identifying, in part, with each. Elizondo's struggle was a struggle to find the "Big Story" that gave sense to his life, the "Big Story" that would allow him to know the structure of his own reality. Elizondo's struggle with his identity came to an unexpected crossroads when he visited the Basilica of Guadalupe in Mexico.

But nothing can surpass my first visit to the Basilica of Our Lady of Guadalupe. It was like entering into the womb of life. I did not then nor do I now have adequate words to explain it all. It was awesome but inviting. It was sacred, but so human—people all around, praying, doing sacrifice, visiting, eating, pick-pocketing. All of life was present there. It attracted people like a huge magnet. (Elizondo 1988, 19)

Our Lady of Guadalupe revealed to Elizondo the founts of his true identity, the possibility of a "Big Story."

Elizondo's struggle with his identity led him to the "little stories" found in the popular religiosity of Our Lady of Guadalupe. Elizondo's assertion of the value of popular religion put him in the center of this hotly contested topic. Popular religion, Elizondo claimed, did not threaten the Church by co-opting its symbols through syncretism or co-opting its message of liberation. Popular religion contained the very mystery of the Church.

POPULAR RELIGION

But what, exactly, is popular religion? Everyone knows what popular religion is, yet no one seems able to define it (Isambert 1982, 21). An example of popular religion can be seen in this account by Fray Francisco de Paredes, the *Predicador General* of St. Martín's Order.

[On the day St. Martín died,] this witness was ordered to guard the body until it was taken to the gravesite. And this witness saw that since four in the morning the whole city of Lima had come together, even people who lived far away, to see the body of said venerable brother fray Martín de Porras; and they would touch their rosaries to his body, and even though they tried to prevent people from cutting pieces of clothing from his body, it could not be prevented and many pieces were cut from his habit. Meanwhile, the body of said venerable brother fray Martín de Porras remained soft and lovely and fragrant.

There are, of course, many other examples. Popular religion, for instance, involves sacred places, magic rites, and exchanges with the dead. Popular religion also involves many Christian feasts: All Saint's Day, Christmas, Easter, patron feasts of cities, and feasts devoted to Mary. Popular religion even involves traditions dealing with life at the local level: baptisms and communions, benedictions of people and harvests, fraternities and processions, images and hymns, relics and *ex voto,* candles and medals, crosses and crucifixes. And, of course, popular religion involves the individual needs of families: marriages and churchings, dying and the dead (Thils 1977, 198). Yet if asked for a definition that would encompass such phenomena, few of us could give a satisfactory answer.

Robert Schreiter suggests the use of contrasts as a means toward defining what is meant by popular religion (Schreiter 1985, 124-5).[5] Official religion, for example, sees popular religion as falling outside its prescribed norms. Official religion endeavors to bring popular religion more in line with its practice. Such might describe the concerns of the Latin American religious right.

Another type of contrast may be made between popular and elite religion. The elite can be a power group or an intellectual group. As such, the popular often includes the poor or the uneducated under its rubric. The popular, in this context, refers to the masses. The elite see the masses as the object of their agenda, passive objects that need to be led or educated. Such might describe the concerns of the Latin American religious left.

A third type of contrast may also be made between esoteric and exoteric knowledge. As such, a select few will be privy to sophisticated religious lore while the outside group is given a less sophisticated and more general version. These contrasts, however, all reflect the concerns of the official side, which sees the popular as a problem. For this reason, popular religion may be hard to define since, in part, it is an object of study by the very elites that consider it a problem.

At first glance, Schreiter's use of contrasts in defining popular religion seems to have taken us to a less-than-helpful conclusion: popular religion may be impossible to define. Nonetheless, one can notice that all the above contrasts have one element in common. Popular religion appears to be a place where passive objects of religion are formed. In other words, people who participate in popular religion are seen to become passive, even mindless, that is, objects—at least to the minds of the official, elite, or esoteric group. This common element, however, does not exhaust the possibilities for a viable definition.

Popular religion, for example, could also be a place where subjects of popular religiosity are formed. In other words, people who participate in popular religion are doing so consciously and with their own particular reasons. Fray Juan Ochoa de Verátesgui, for example, tells the following "little story" about St. Martín.

> And this witness, seeing one morning said venerable brother fray Martín de Porras occupied in cleaning the toilets of the convent, which he came to do every morning, even while staying at the house of the Lord Archbishop of Mexico Don Feliciano de Vega, who was at that time in the city sick and had asked as a special favor for [St. Martín] to assist him, this witness asked said venerable brother fray Martín de Porras: "Brother fray Martín, ¿Is it not better to be in the house of the Lord Archbishop of Mexico than in the toilets of the convent?" To which said servant of God responded what saintly King David had said: *Elegi abjectus esse in domo Dei mei magis quam habitare in tabernaculis peccatorum.* "Father fray Juan, I prefer a little time spent in this work than many days spent in the house of the Lord Archbishop."

St. Martín quoted Psalm 84:10: "For a day in your courts is better than a thousand elsewhere. I would rather be a doorkeeper in the house of my God than live in the tents of wickedness" (NRSV translation).

St. Martín, of course, was a doorkeeper in the convent. It was his most treasured identity and is celebrated popularly by the symbol of the broom with which he is always portrayed. Clearly, there is a sense of resistance and challenge in the story dealing with the archbishop's illness. As such, this "little story" does not present St. Martín as some passive object. Indeed, as a healer, St. Martín actively takes charge of his life and the lives of others.

Perhaps a better way to explore the definition of popular religion is to take the phrase apart. The word *popular,* for instance, can be looked at by itself profitably. As such, *popular* implies opposition to some class or some group. But opposed in what way? The answer to this question owes a great debt to the work of Antonio Gramsci.

ANTONIO GRAMSCI

Many consider Antonio Gramsci one of the most innovative Marxist thinkers since Lenin. He developed the concept of the "subaltern" classes. A subaltern class lies at the periphery of the dominant power-bearing group in society, but not because of force and coercion, as classical Marxism insisted. There were more subtle (and powerful) forces at work—such as the force of the cultural unconscious, for example—that shaped the worldview of popular culture so it might coincide with a repressive status quo.

Gramsci called this force "Egenomia" or hegemony. Hegemony refers to a dominant concept of reality that informs a society's way of life. Such a view of reality dominates all the institutions and manifestations of that society. Hegemony involves an element of direction and control that is not necessarily conscious.

Yet hegemony is not an all-powerful arm of the state. It does serve the interests of the state, but hegemony is, in a sense, also an agreement between two classes. No regime can rely solely on direct coercion. It must find popular support by means of ideological control or hegemony. As such, hegemony is not so much a contrast but a two-edged sword, a process of accommodation and resistance by both dominant and subaltern classes through which a status quo is reached.[6] Take, for example, the testimony of Fray Cipriano de Medina, holder of the chair of theology in the *Real Universidad* of Lima.

This witness says, that, in the year 1639, the Archbishop of Mexico, Don Feliciano de Vega, while visiting the city [of Lima] came down with a serious illness with fevers and a great pain on his side of which many doctors in the city came to cure him. And having bled him many times and applying various medicines, not only did he not get better but his illness grew so worse that after many days, one Sunday in the morning all the doctors gave up on him and ordered that he be given the Viaticum and Extreme Unction and that a will be made. This witness being there and being his nephew and saddened by his danger told him: "Why has your Illustrous Lordship not called on our fray Martín de Porras, our nurse, who, no doubt, would have healed you?" "You're right," said the Lord Archbishop, "Go, nephew, to the convent and tell the Father Provincial to send him to me." And this witness said to him: "When he comes, order him to put his hand where your pain is and you will see how he heals you." This he could see because of the experience with said brother in the convent with the great works the Lord had done and continued to do through him.

Hurriedly arriving at the convent, this witness passed on the request to the Father Provincial who was Father fray Luis de la Rasa who died five years ago and who, with due dispatch, sent brothers out to find said brother fray Martín throughout all the convent. And not having appeared between seven to nine in the morning, it was remembered that it was a day of communion, and in those days he was never found for he retired where no one could see him, to commune alone with God. And the Father Provincial being very upset that he was not found, this witness said to him: "Honorable Father, order him in obedience to appear here and you shall see how soon we shall have him." Everyone was amazed at such a rare happening that at the moment of ordering in obedience to appear, said brother fray Martín walked in through the sacristy. Father Provincial then told him to go with this witness to the house of said Archbishop and do whatever he tells him.

And having gone and entering the room where said Archbishop was lying in the presence of his whole family and others began to reprimand him because he had not visited him. And said fray Martín threw himself upon the ground, without saying a word, as is the custom in religious life and in the special constitution of his [order] to listen to reprimands this way, [the Archbishop] made signs for him to get up and ordered him to come to the bed. To which [St. Martín] responded: "What does a Prince want with the hand of a poor mulatto lay brother?" To which the said Archbishop responded, "Has not your Prelate ordered you to do what I tell you?" And he said: "Yes sir." "Then put your hand on this side where I have the pain." And fray Martín putting his hand on his side, the Archbishop, immediately, felt the pain to be gone. And knowing what had happened [St. Martín] began to be disturbed and his face turned red and began to sweat profusely and said: "Is it enough, Sir?" And the Archbishop replied: "Leave it there where you have placed it." And being like this for a while, [the Archbishop] found himself relieved, free of the fever, and now only had to rest to the great admiration of all who were present and specially of the doctors who returned in the afternoon and with one voice acclaimed the wonder that God had done through his servant.

At first glance, St. Martín's humility may seem debasing in front of the powerful. Yet, as a subaltern reading, this humility is a double-edged sword. It is the archbishop who seeks a favor from St. Martín, not the other way around. St. Martín's question, "What does a Prince want with the hand of a poor mulatto lay brother?" is full of irony and challenge. The archbishop, after all, is dying. St. Martín has the power to prevent it. The "little story" may be a story about a miraculous healing of an archbishop, but it is also a story about the power of St. Martín, a humble servant of God who cleaned toilets yet was sought after by a mighty archbishop.

Antonio Gramsci's concept of hegemony avoids the idea of the popular as an object of the powerful, official, elite, or specialized and brings to it the idea of subject formation. Subject formation allows a view of the popular as a dynamic process rather than some passive object. Nonetheless, Gramsci's hegemony can lead to some simplistic or unrealistic interpretations of the popular. Sociologists Rowe and Schelling point out three persistent interpretations of the popular made by those who assume the existence of a hegemony between dominant and subaltern social groups.

One interpretation arose with Romanticism. This interpretation sees an authentic rural culture threatened by industrialization and its mass media. A "pure" country culture is in danger of being degraded or forgotten through the pressures of the ever-invasive city or its mass media. The victim of such invasion is often described as the experience of community. The problem with this interpretation is the assumption that traditional and modern worlds cannot co-exist. The popular, however, participate in both worlds and have done so for some time.

The second interpretation sees the popular as inevitably moving toward a mass culture associated with the large modern cities of First World capitalist countries. Such a view has been seen as either a tragedy or a solution. The problem with this interpretation is the assumption that the popular do not possess an inventiveness of their own capable of bringing about a modernity that is different from the mass culture of the urban First World.

The third interpretation sees the popular as moving toward liberation expressed by some utopian goal. The popular, in this view, contain within themselves the resources for imagining an alternative future society. The problem with this interpretation is the assumption that one can observe, as if from some ideal place, what is able to contribute (or not) to this emerging utopian future. Unfortunately, the elements that make for a utopic future present themselves in a less-than-clear manner.

Rowe and Schelling (1991, 10, 12) suggest a way of interpreting the popular that avoids these problematic assumptions. "One way of developing [Gramsci's] insights is to take popular culture not as a given view of the world but as a space or series of spaces where popular subjects are formed. . . . it is the decisive area where social conflicts are experienced and evaluated." Defining the popular in this way, Rowe and Schelling make clear that the popular is not an object, a meaning, or even a social group. This has certain implications. First, the notion of the popular as a site (a place located in social experience) or more accurately, a series of dispersed sites, opposes the idea of populism, that is, the notion of nation as a single body.

Moreover, the notion of dispersed sites is not the same as pluralism. Pluralism gives the state the anything but neutral role of mediating a plurality of interests. Such intervention of the state actually homogenizes cultural subjects, a process inimical to hegemony, in which cultural subjects are formed.[7]

Perhaps the most interesting implication questions the assumption that the role of subaltern groups is necessarily one of resistance to dominant authority. To describe the popular through the simple language of conformity or resistance to power reduces the meaning of the issues involved. Actually, both resistance and conformity occur simultaneously in the popular. Bishop and layperson both participate in popular religion. The eyewitnesses at St. Martín's beatification process included a wide range of people from every class and race: from Francisca, an African slave, to a captain of the police force, to a theologian from the *Real Universidad* of Lima. The point of Rowe and Schelling's interpretation of the popular is that the opposition implied in the popular is not opposition as engaged in by collective subjects but opposition as "modes of conflict which link discourse and practice" (1991, 11).

The site definition of Rowe and Schelling allows keeping the best in the subaltern concept while avoiding simplistic hegemonies that do not reflect reality. The site definition also gives clarity to what is meant and not meant by popular. The popular, for example, does not mean a Romantic concept of people, a pristine unified social body. Neither does it mean a noble primitive group that's been left behind by technological or capitalist growth. Nor does popular necessarily mean an oppressed group in constant resistance to an oppressor. What popular does mean is a site or series of sites where conflict is experienced and evaluated, where popular subjects are formed.

Rowe and Schelling's understanding of popular makes it possible to define popular religion in a new and perhaps more useful way. Popular religion, by analogy, becomes a site or series of sites where religious conflicts are experienced and evaluated, where religious subjects are formed. By not treating popular religion as an object, a meaning, or a social group, this definition goes a long way toward representing the phenomena of popular religion. Yet even this powerful definition does not suffice for the professional theologian. Elizondo's case for the value of the "little stories" of popular religion rested on the assumption that the "Big Story" lay behind. For the theologian, this means the "Big Story" of faith, the "Big Story" that brings understanding to faith.

RELIGION

The issue of faith may be approached through the term *religion.* The word *religion* derives from two Latin words: *religio*, which means reverence or devotion, and *ligare*, which means to fasten or bind together. The meanings of the word range from "a state of life bound by monastic vows" to "recognition on the part of man of some higher unseen power as having control of his destiny" (*Oxford English Dictionary*).

The word *religion*, however, also signifies a long-standing issue between the academy and the Church. Jacob Preus, for example, makes the distinction between theology and the study of religion. Preus goes on to demonstrate that the "study of religion" was born in the Enlightenment through a decisive assumption that

> religion could be understood . . . without the magisterial guidance of religious authorities and, more radically, without "conversion" [that is,] confessional or metaphysical commitments about its causes *different* from the assumptions one might use to understand and explain other realms of culture. Contrary to the claim of classical Western theology, this new tradition claimed and claims that it is not necessary to believe

in order to understand—indeed, that suspension of belief is probably a condition for understanding. (1987, x)

Such an assumption was made possible through three significant events of the sixteenth century: the religious wars of the Reformation; the encounter of non-European (or non-Classical) cultures; and the early achievements of the natural sciences. These events, asserts Preus, led to a debate about religion that undermined the claims of theology to be the proper perspective by which to study religious phenomena. Indeed, the word *religion* only begins to appear in the modern sense in 1535. As such, Preus sees theology and the study of religion as two rival paradigms.

The merits of Preus' proposal lies in uncovering what is at stake for a theologian such as Elizondo, who wants to study popular religion. Such a theologian must be prepared to cross academic turfs. For anthropologists, religion encompasses a multitude of phenomena. The anthropologist Shweder puts it (1991, 30):

For anthropologists the confrontation with diversity in belief, desire, and practice can be a radical one. Here is a short list of the things we can observe out there in the world of human beings if we look in the right places and with the right clearance: people hunting for witches, exorcising demons, propitiating dead ancestors, sacrificing animals to hungry gods, sanctifying temples, waiting for messiahs, scapegoating their sins, consulting the stars, decoding their dreams, flagellating themselves in public, prohibiting the eating of pork (or dog, or beef, or all swarming things except locusts, crickets, and grasshoppers), wandering on pilgrimage from one dilapidated shrine to the next, abstaining from sex on the day of the full moon, refusing to be in the same room with their wife's elder sister, matting their hair with cow dung, isolating women during menstruation, seeking salvation by meditating naked in a cave for several years, and so on and on.

This bewildering variety of religious phenomena has led modern anthropologists to define religion as some combination of Edward Tylor's (1873) "belief in Spiritual Beings" and Emile Durkheim's (1915) "system of beliefs and practices relative to sacred things" (Pandian 1991). More recently, the importance of symbols have entered into the academic definition of religion. A theologian wishing to reflect on popular religion must be aware of the issues involved in such definitions. The issue of faith is at stake. Can the theological locus of faith be retained amid the various academic understandings of religion?

Paul Tillich, the great theologian, once defined religion as "directedness towards the Unconditioned" and theology as those statements "which deal with their object insofar as it can become a matter of being or not-being for us," that is, our "ultimate concern" (1951, 14). Through his existential formulation, Tillich believed he had found a way in which a theologian could speak meaningfully about religion. Tillich's definition had a wide impact. Sociologist Robert Bellah, for example, comes close to Tillich's definition when he defines religion as "a set of symbolic forms and acts which relate man to the ultimate conditions of his existence" (1964). I find Tillich's insights crucial for the theologian who wants to cross other turfs in theological reflection and essential in arriving at an understanding of faith in terms of the "Big Story."

There are some problems to overcome, however. Tillich's "Unconditioned" is the antithesis of communications. The Unconditioned is not a story that can be told. Rather it is the place where storytelling ends. As such, it seems the very opposite of the "Big Story." Nonetheless, there is another way to look at the Unconditioned. The Unconditioned presents ultimate reality to the individual as the total absence or failure of communication. The "Big Story," on the other hand, presents ultimate reality to the individual as the fullness of communication. Both express the notion of faith. The "Big Story" does so through a positive relationship with respect to the act of communication; the Unconditioned as a negative relationship. Thus, they are flip sides of the same coin: the appropriation of a message (negative or positive) about ultimate reality.

As such, a tentative definition of faith may be hazarded. Faith is *the personal appropriation by an individual of a "Big Story."* This, I believe, gathers Tillich's insights and places them in a positive relationship to the act of communication. As such, it allows the notion of faith to be used in an understanding of popular religion. Because this notion of faith is placed in a positive relationship with the act of communication, this definition is not an apology for a personal religion. Indeed, at heart in this definition is the assumption that "Big Stories" come to us through social and cultural communication systems. Nonetheless, such "Big Stories" must be appropriated consciously and willingly by some individual. Only with this assumption can the full breadth of the diversity of religious phenomena described by Shweder be explained.[8]

TOWARD A DEFINITION

Such an understanding of faith, in turn, allows for a working definition of popular religion. *Popular religion is a site, or a series of sites, in which faith is challenged, interpreted, and made one's own.* Such a definition highlights the notion of challenge or struggle implicit in the subaltern concept yet captures its theological significance with the notion of faith. Indeed, partakers of popular religion may be seen as putting their faith "on the line." Disease, family unrest, or even social conflict may be typical motivations for popular religious practice, but they also happen to be challenges to faith, a struggle where faith is at stake. The result of that struggle is a reinterpretation or reevaluation of that faith, of the "Big Story" that lies behind that faith which is then willingly, consciously, made one's own.

Making faith one's own may be seen as a goal of the Church or as a challenge to her. Perhaps it is here where most suspicion of popular religion occurs, for in making faith one's own, there is a danger that such a faith may not correspond with that of the official institution. Indeed, this does happen. On the other hand, without making faith one's own, there can be no authentic participation in the "Big Story" of the official institution. This, I believe, is the significance of popular religion for the Church. Popular religion is a way in which the faith of its members becomes authenticated. Popular religion is a crucible in which the faith of the Church becomes incarnated. It is a place where the "Big Story" carried by official tradition is made possible through the "little stories" of the popular.

Defining popular religion as the site or series of sites where faith is challenged, interpreted, and made one's own reveals the significance of Virgilio Elizondo's contribution to theological reflection. Popular religion is an essential component of the Church. Through it, her members incarnate the faith received through the Church and make it authentic, that is, make it one's own. As such, this process of making faith one's own reveals a "Big Story" behind the challenges and reevaluations to faith taking place in popular religion. Making faith one's own generates the "little stories" that make possible the "Big Story" of the Church and her faith.

Now the question asked at the beginning can be answered. Moreover, it is a question a theologian can answer and indeed must answer. The "little stories" are manifestations of faith seeking understanding. They can be found wherever faith is challenged, reinterpreted, and made one's own. One such place is the beatification process of St. Martín de Porres that took place between 1660-1664 in colonial Lima.

THE BEATIFICATION AND CANONIZATION PROCESS

The *New Catholic Encyclopedia* describes canonization as, "an act or definitive sentence by which the pope decrees that a servant of God, member of the Catholic Church and already declared blessed, be inscribed in the book of saints and be venerated in the universal Church with the cult given to all saints."

This definition makes it clear that the canonization process has as one of its goals to uphold an individual as a model of orthodoxy. This goal was not always so clear. The early history of the cult of saints was more a matter of acclamation than process. The martyrdom of charismatic individuals gave them popular acclaim to the title of saint. After the Diocletian persecution, when Emperor Constantine made Christianity the Empire's religion, the cult of martyrs became transformed into the cult of saints (*see* Brown 1981). Since then, "making saints" shifted from a process of popular acclamation to a process more akin to litigation. As Molinari puts it (McDonald 1967a, 55-6):

> In the first centuries the popular fame or the *vox populi* represented in practice the only criterion by which a person's holiness was ascertained. A new element was gradually introduced, namely the intervention of the ecclesiastical authority, i.e., of the competent bishop . . . The transition from episcopal to papal canonization came about somewhat casually. The custom was gradually introduced of having recourse to the pope in order to receive a formal approval of the canonization . . . Through a gradual multiplication of the interventions of the Roman pontiffs, papal canonization received a more definite structure and juridical value. Procedural norms were formulated, and such canonical processes became the main source of investigation into the saint's life and miracles.

By the eleventh century, Pope Urban II specified witnesses to the miracles occasioned by the saints-to-be. In 1234, Gregory IX, a legal-minded Pope, set up the existing process for determining sainthood. This process required witnesses and depositions.

The sixteenth century, due to the Reformation and in the wake of the Council of Trent, called into question the whole matter of the veneration of saints (Kemp 1948, 141). In 1588, the Congregation of Sacred Rites and Ceremonies, a standing committee of cardinals whose responsibilities included canonizations, was formed. In 1625 and 1634, Pope Urban VIII made the procedures increasingly strict and formal. A distinction between saints and "beati" was made sharper. A wait of 50 years after death had to ensue before proceedings could start. In 1734, Canon Lawyer Prospero Lambertini and, later, Benedict XIV made the process even more strict. Sanctity was defined in the Aristotelian-Thomist concept of a "heroic" degree of virtue, the procedures became more bureaucratic, and recruitment procedures were made more formal and uniform (Kemp 1948, 141).

By the time of St. Martín, the strict requirements of Benedict XIV had not yet taken shape. Nonetheless, a juridical process was in place. Canonization could not begin without a preliminary beatification process. The first step in the beatification process involved the appointment by the Ordinary bishop of a Procurator General or Postulator to be a coordinator of the saint-to-be's cause. The first process was known as *Processus de non cultu*, convened to determine if a cult existed around the saint-to-be. (This was a requirement insisted on by Urban VIII.) If no previous cult was shown to exist, the next two processes could be started, the *Processus ordinarius*, or Informative process, known in Spanish as the *Proceso Sumario,* and the *Processus in specie*, or Apostolic process.

The *Processus ordinarius* (Ordinary process) was an investigation in general (*in genere*) of the life, deeds, and popular support of the individual in question for the purpose of soliciting a formal inquiry by the Sacred Congregation of Rites of the Apostolic See. The Ordinary process is similar to a grand jury, in which a judgment is made as to whether a case merits a formal trial. There was nothing informal about the Informative process, however. Witnesses were called, oaths were taken, and specific questions (a total of 20) were asked (*see Proceso,* 75-7). The current code for conducting the Informative process is similar to the one used in St. Martín's time (McDonald 1967a, 56):

Following the death of a person who has lived an exemplary Christian life, the so-called "fame of sanctity" or "fame of martyrdom" may spread in an ever-increasing manner, together with the conviction that by appealing to his intercession, special favors will be granted by God. The bishop of the diocese where the person died, may, if he deems it opportune, institute a process. A tribunal is established to interrogate witnesses in order to gather evidence of a juridical character, which the Congregation of Rites will use in ascertaining whether or not there exists *de facto* a fame of sanctity and, if so, its foundation and extent. This process on the repute of sanctity or martyrdom is called ordinary, because it is instituted by authority of the ordinary of the place. It is said to be informative, since it furnishes the Holy See with the information necessary to determine the advisability of formally introducing the cause, in order to verify whether the servant of God exercised virtues in a heroic manner or whether he died for the faith.

The *Introduction of the Cause* was the next step after the Ordinary Process. A brief is prepared by one of the advocate-procurators of the Congregation of Rites, based on the testimonies and documents available and aimed at proving the existence of a true reputation for sanctity before the Congregation. After the Congregation examines the brief, the general promoter of the faith proposes his objections to the brief in a document entitled *Animadversiones*. These objections are responded to by the postulator of the cause. All this material is then published as one document, the *Positio,* which is examined by the Congregation of Rites. If the cardinals of the Congregation approve, the Pope may then call for the next process, which involves an investigation of the heroic virtue in detail (*in specie*). This process is called the Apostolic process and is under the jurisdiction of the Holy See (McDonald 1967a, 57).

The Apostolic process is similar to the Informative or Ordinary Process. Witnesses are called and interrogated as to the virtues and sanctity of the individual's life. The testimony is sent back to the Congregation of Rites, which examines it, raises objections to it, and asks for a response to these objections. This process can take place several times. The final stage takes place with the Congregation *coram Sanctissimo* (in the presence of the Holy Father) to make a final determination. If the Holy Father approves, the individual is canonized, that is, written into the canon of saints.

One problem with the canonization process is that many of the eyewitnesses who could give the kind of detail needed for the Apostolic stage of the process would have died by this time. Thus the Ordinary process often recorded great detail for a future Apostolic process, even though technically it was not necessary. This was the case in St. Martín's beatification process. Although preparation for the beatification process for St. Martín was approved on November 8, 1657 (only 18 years after St. Martín's death), the actual process did not start until 1660.[9] Close to a hundred witnesses were interrogated in great detail. Apparently the good people of Lima wanted to capture as much detail as possible, in case the Apostolic process would not take place in the near future.

The Ordinary process of St. Martín is an excellent site for the telling of "little stories."[10] First, the eyewitness depositions were relatively fresh, part of a cultural experience that was present and available for articulation. Second, the beatification of a New World mulatto would be unique. The depositions given by the eyewitnesses would address the implicit question of the humanity of this New World mulatto.

The beatification of St. Martín not only involved a process of popular acclamation. It also involved an Old World central bureaucracy asked to judge whether this New World individual "played by the rules" expected of Old World saints. As such, the process appears similar to the "project of language" or "story" that Jonathan Z. Smith talked about. The people of Lima who were affected by the life and deeds of St. Martín would now try to articulate a New World reality by recounting "little stories" about a new human phenomenon of the New World, the mestizo mulatto St. Martín.

As such, it was a faith challenged, an exercise of the imagination, a search for new concepts in terms of older ones. Moreover, it was a process not only to make St. Martín the Church's own, but also one's own, for the people of Lima found their own faith renewed, become authentic, in the very stories they told. For these reasons, the stories found in the beatification process of St. Martín may be seen as "little stories" making possible a "Big Story." Having found the "little stories," the next challenge is how to read them.

3

Reading the "Little Story"

It is one thing to find the "little stories." It is another to be able to read them. The "little stories" are at the same time intensely personal yet cosmic, highly individual yet socially encompassing. Such is the case with the "little stories" of St. Martín. If they were to be read as personal anecdotes, one might miss their import as the eccentric fantasies of an individual. If they were to be read as a manifestation of a social or cultural phenomenon, one might dismiss their meaning as the self-interest of a class or the passive product of socioeconomic forces.

Yet neither of these extreme perspectives truly reads the "little story." How would either of these perspectives read the following "little story" of Francisco Ortiz, who knew St. Martín because he became sick one day and was tended by St. Martín? Sr. Ortiz testified:

> One day speaking with said venerable brother fray Martín de Porras, much praise was given a certain lay brother of his Order who taught reading, writing, and every good doctrine to twenty-four orphans in the city of Manila [Phillipines] . . . This lay brother was well known and respected by all in Manila because of his good works . . . When said venerable brother fray Martín de Porras heard this good account of the lay brother, he showed signs that he wanted to meet this lay brother. This witness does not know if said venerable brother saw said lay brother in Manila because [St. Martín] never mentioned it, and the witness never asked him. What he did see was that not three days later, this witness went to speak with said venerable brother fray Martín de Porras and found him very happy and joyful speaking the Chinese tongue, which this witness understood, and thus, it seemed to him, that

25

[St. Martín] must have seen and spoken with [the lay brother in Manila], how or through what means this witness did not know.

Was Sr. Ortiz some eccentric fool, or was his testimony serving some class or social self-interest? Such assumptions do not read this "little story" but rather dismiss it.

St. Martín's ability to cross boundaries—geographical and otherwise—does say something about the social and economic conditions of his day. And Sr. Ortiz' account could only have been told in his own eccentric way. Nonetheless, behind the eccentricity and the socioeconomic context lies a "Big Story" of faith. The "little stories," above all, must be read as manifestations in which faith is challenged, reinterpreted, and made one's own. It was not until the past decade, however, that the means for such a reading was spelled out by two pioneer "little story" tellers: Virgilio Elizondo and Robert Schreiter.

"READING" OUR LADY OF GUADALUPE

Popular religion as a site where faith is challenged, interpreted, and made one's own allows one to appreciate the attraction the popular Church of San Antonio had for Elizondo. His search for identity was also a struggle of faith, a struggle to find his role in the "Big Story." He found the natural site for such a struggle in popular religion, in the "little stories" of Our Lady of Guadalupe. One such story is narrated by Elizondo (1977, 25-33):

In 1531, ten years after the conquest, an event happened whose origins are clouded in mystery, yet its effects have been monumental and ongoing . . . According to the legend, as Juan Diego, a Christianized Indian of common status, was going from his home in the "barriada" near Tepeyac, he heard beautiful music. As he approached the source of the music, a lady appeared to him and speaking in Nahuatl, the language of the conquered, she commanded Juan Diego to go to the palace of the archbishop of Mexico at Tlatelolco and to tell him that the Virgin Mary, "Mother of the true God, through whom one lives" wanted a temple to be built at that site so that in it she "can show and give forth all my love, compassion, help, and defence to all the inhabitants of this land . . . to hear their lamentations and remedy their miseries, pain, and sufferings." After two unsuccessful attempts to convince the bishop of the Lady's authenticity, the Virgin wrought a miracle. She sent Juan Diego to pick roses in a place where only desert plants existed. She arranged the roses on his cloak and sent him to the archbishop with the sign he had demanded. As Juan Diego unfolded his cloak in the presence of the archbishop, the roses fell to the ground and the image of the Virgin appeared on his cloak.

Having found his "little story," Elizondo faced the problem of how to read it, that is, how to discover the meaning of the "little story" and give it thematic or systematic coherence. But where to begin?

It became clear to Elizondo that one must begin with the cultural categories of the "little stories" themselves. What for the Spanish was "an apparition for the conquered and dying Mexican nation" was for Juan Diego the birth of a new civilization (Elizondo 1977, 126). This suggested to Elizondo that the key to reading the "little stories" lay in the symbolic character rooted in the culture. Elizondo thus attempted to read the "little story" by paying attention to its symbolic-cultural dimension (1977, 126-28).

Upon reading the legend, the first striking detail is that Juan Diego heard beautiful music, which alone was enough to establish the heavenly origin of the Lady. For the Indians, music was the medium of divine communication. The Lady appeared on the sacred hill of Tepeyac, one of the four principal sacrificial sites in Meso America. It was the sanctuary of Tonantzin, the Indian virgin mother of the gods. The dress was a pale red, the colour of the spilled blood of sacrifices and the colour of Huitzilopopchtli, the god who gave and preserved life. The blood of the Indians had been spilled on Mexican soil and fertilized mother earth, and now something new came forth. Red was also the colour for the East, the direction from which the sun arose victorious after it had died for the night. The predominant colour of the portrait is the blue-green of the mantle, which was the royal colour of the Indian gods. It was also the colour of Ometéotl, the origin of all natural forces. In the colour psychology of the native world, blue-green stood at the centre of the cross of opposing forces and signified the force unifying the opposing tensions at work in the world . . . The Lady wore the black band of maternity around her waist, the sign that she was with child. She was offering her child to the New World. The Lady was greater than the greatest in the native pantheon because she hid the sun but did not extinguish it. The sun god was their principal deity, and she was more powerful. The Lady was also greater than their moon god, for she stood upon the moon, yet did not crush it. However, great as this Lady was, she was not a goddess. She wore no mask as the Indian gods did, and her vibrant, compassionate face in itself told anyone who looked upon it that she was the compassionate mother.

Yet such a reading was not satisfying. Behind the symbolic meanings of the "little stories" lay a history. This history, however, was more than a social or cultural history. The symbols of the "little stories" were intricately tied to the history that had led to their telling. It was then that Elizondo realized that symbols also have a history. They are not made arbitrarily but emerge from the violent and unequal encounter of cultures. The full meaning of the "little story" of Guadalupe rests not only on its symbols but in the history that gave rise to those symbols.

Elizondo did a second analysis. To the symbolic-cultural analysis, he applied a second analysis focusing on the sociohistorical dimension of the "little story" of Guadalupe (1977, 130-31).

> Not only did the Lady leave a powerful message in the image, but the credentials she chose to present herself to the New World were equally startling. For the bishop, the roses from the desert were a startling phenomenon; for the Indians, they were the sign of life . . . At the time of the apparition, the Spanish were building churches over the ruins of the Aztec temples. The past grandeur and power of Tenochtitlán-Tlatelolco (the original name for present-day Mexico City) was being transformed into the glory of New Spain, which was to supplant native Mexico. The tearing down and the building up was symbolic of the deeper struggle to destroy a people, even if the intention was to rebuild it. Juan Diego dared to go to the city of power and with supernatural authority—the native lady had commanded—he demanded that the powerful change their plans and build a temple—a symbol of a new way of life—not within the grandeur of the city in accordance with the plans of Spain, but within the *barriada* of Tepeyac in accordance with the desires of the native people of this land. The hero of the story is a simple conquered Indian from the barriada who is a symbol of the poor and oppressed refusing to be destroyed by the dominant group. The purpose of the story was to lead the archbishop, the symbol of the new Spanish power group, to a conversion so as to turn the attention of the conquering group from building up the rich and powerful center of governments, knowledge and religion, to the periphery of society where the people continued to live in poverty and misery.

The full significance of the "little story" of Guadalupe now emerges. The Virgin of Guadalupe grounds the identity of those who live in the violent and unequal encounter of cultures. The "little story" of the Virgin of Guadalupe reveals the "Big Story" of a new humanity emerging from the violent and unequal encounter of cultures that began in Mexico in 1531. The "Big Story" tells of a new humanity that is breaking ancient human structures contributing to division and separateness. This new humanity will celebrate its particularities even as it breaks through to a new connectedness. The request for a temple was "not just for a building where her image could be venerated but for a new way of life. It would express continuity with the past, but radically transcend that past" (Elizondo 1977, 29). The people of Mexico had not been abandoned by God before the Europeans had come. God had lived in their symbols and in their history. Their "little stories" merged with the Europeans' "little stories" to make possible the "Big Story" of an experience of grace that grounded the meaning of their identity.

Elizondo showed a new generation of Hispanic theologians the importance of the "little stories." Elizondo was also one of the first to actually devise a method by which to read them. Elizondo's dual use of symbolic-cultural and sociohistorical analyses of the "little story" opened a door through which new methods could expand and fortify his pioneering work. One such method is the semiotics of culture developed by Robert Schreiter.

ROBERT SCHREITER

Robert Schreiter is another pioneer "little story" teller. Schreiter began his search for the "Big Story" amid the overwhelming variety of worldviews present in the growing number of new Christian churches. Schreiter recognized that a new shift in theological perspective has been emerging since the 1950s. This shift originated in the reflection of Christians belonging to the new churches of Asia and Africa and Christians belonging to the marginated classes such as those found in Latin America.

Schreiter found that all these churches shared some common elements in their respective perspectives. Above all, new questions were being asked, questions arising from the particularity and contingency of the local circumstances. These new questions impacted on the question of "specialist" language. As Schreiter noted, "it was becoming increasingly evident that the theologies once thought to have a universal, and even enduring or perennial character (such as neo-scholastic Thomism in Catholicism or neo-orthodoxy in Protestantism) were but regional expressions of certain cultures" (1985, 3).

The growing awareness by a global society of the role culture plays in understanding led to a questioning of the nature of the specialist's understanding itself. Specialists, after all, are also creatures of culture. The specialists' respective cultures provide the concepts through which they themselves must understand their world.

This challenge to the relevancy of specialist language purporting to be universal yet based on the contingency of culture opened the door to a new awareness by the local churches of Africa, Asia, and Latin America. A new kind of Christian identity was being born, one not solely dependent on specialist understanding. The understanding of the specialists of the Church, theologians and Church officials, must now be subjected to three areas particularly sensitive to the local Church: context, procedure, and history.

The awareness that starting reflection before first analyzing the context leads to irrelevancy or, worse, ideological manipulation, underscored the need for sensitivity to context. Such dependence on context means that meaning and the production of that meaning is essential to the theological enterprise. Procedure now becomes an important element of theological reflection. How a specialist arrives at his specialized language determines how meaningful (and how relevant) his or her language is. This means that theological procedure, in this new perspective, must respect the way meaning is produced locally. Like a set of falling dominos, a reexamination of theological procedure led to another realization. The received theology of many new Christian churches did not account for local histories. Histories of suffering, histories of when Christianity was not the religion of the people, and the ambiguity of the history of how the gospel was received by these new churches all took on essential importance as the new churches began their own theological reflection.

What, then, is the role of the specialist, if he or she is to take this new perspective with its new sensitivities seriously? Schreiter (1985, 50) suggests that:

> Our task is, after all, one of listening to a culture; and listening entails a certain discipline. On the one hand, it is not merely a passive undertaking; listening is an involvement in an exchange. But at the same time listeners must not forget that they do not control the direction of the exchange. Listeners are called to follow the direction of the speaker, and to move more deeply into the speaker's reality. Listeners must be aware of the structures that inform their listening, and be able to recognize when those structures no longer adequately give form to what they are hearing. To grow in the understanding of a culture is to learn the ascesis of listening and to stand open to the transformations that can ensue from it.

Schreiter suggests, in essence, that the "little stories" of a culture make possible the telling of the "Big Story." But how does a specialist approach these "little stories"? How does a specialist begin to understand the universal import inherent in a culture's "little stories"?

THE SEMIOTICS OF CULTURE

Anyone who has traveled to other countries knows that sometimes the fastest way to communicate is not through language but through signs. You can, using a Cantonese Chinese-English dictionary, try to communicate to a store clerk in Shanghai what you want to buy at his store—or you can point to the object of your desire. Pointing to an object is the essence of sign. Signs and culture naturally correlate. Signs form the basis for communication in any culture. They are more basic than language.[1] Many anthropologists, missionaries, and communication specialists have focused their attention on this natural correlation between signs and culture. Indeed, the anthropologist Clifford Geertz (1973, 5) saw culture as essentially a system of signs, "webs of significance" spun by human beings.

Robert Schreiter recognized the natural correlation between signs and culture as the key by which one could read nontraditional stories, the "little stories" of a culture. Schreiter, like Geertz, saw culture as a sphere of meaning in which a system of signs signifies an underlying meaning expressing a cultural message. Such a system of signs could be thought of as a cultural "text" in analogy to a linguistic or written text. Instead of spoken or written words, a cultural text could be nonverbal and thus nontraditional. Schreiter suggested that a culture's "little stories" could be "read" through this new procedure called the semiotics of culture.

Semiotics, *per se*, studies signs and the relationships between signs.[2] A sign points to something besides itself. From peacock feathers to the color green, from crossing yourself when entering a door to saying thanks—all these may be signs. A precise definition, however, may be found in Charles Peirce's definition of sign as *something which stands to somebody for something in some respect or capacity*.[3] Signs relate to one another by means of codes. Codes are a necessary element in creating a message with signs. Consider, for example, the meaning of a man's rapidly contracting right eyelid.[4] In a doctor's office, such a contraction might be interpreted as simply a twitch. In a singles' bar, the interpretation might be akin to a suggestive wink. The difference between a twitch and a wink is vast and reveals the existence of social codes that allow the interpretation of the barrage of signs cultural human beings are exposed to.

Signs, codes, and messages make up the basic elements of a semiotics of culture. Signs, in the semiotics of culture, connect to one another by means of codes or rules which, in "creative collaboration," produce the messages in a culture. A linguistic metaphor for this process would be a sentence. If words are signs and a meaningful sentence made of a string of these words is a message, then the rules, the grammar that strings together such words into that sentence, are the codes. When these signs, codes, and messages relate to one another in such a way as to form a unified, self-consistent whole, they form a cultural text. In a cultural text one has signs instead of words, codes instead of grammar, and messages instead of sentences. Such a "text," although not traditional, may nonetheless be read by anyone familiar with the signs, codes, and messages that make up the words, grammar, and sentences of the text. The task of a semiotic analysis of culture consists in reading the cultural text, which means "locate its signs, the codes that place the signs in dynamic interaction, and the messages that are conveyed" (Schreiter 1985, 61).

At this point, however, something else must be mentioned. A semiotics of culture is more than the semiotics familiar to linguists and structuralists.

A semiotics of culture concerns itself more with a "way of life than a view of life" (Schreiter 1985, 33). As such, the straightforward message of the linguistic text is not an appropriate metaphor to describe the messages of a way of life. Differences of color, shading, and nuance distinguish messages in the violent and unequal encounter of cultures from a linguistic message. A visual metaphor capable of expressing ways of life, rather than views of life, is more appropriate.

THE CULTURAL MOSAIC

Several years ago, a striking cartoon appeared in one of Chicago's major newspapers. It pretended to celebrate Chicago's self-consciousness as a "city of neighborhoods." This self-image was given form as a map of Chicago's neighborhoods, each clearly marked by strong lines reflecting their respective boundaries. The cartoon, however, showed its true intent when, on further inspection, the reader saw each neighborhood labeled as either an "us" or "them." Moreover, opposite each "us" neighborhood, a "them" neighborhood stood in stark contrast. The message, of course, communicated that Chicago's neighborhoods identified themselves as much by differentiating themselves from some other neighborhood as by any self-proclaimed character proper to that particular neighborhood. The other message, unfortunately, was that such a process of identity formation was one of conflict. The study of the semiotics of culture, when applied to the violent and unequal encounter of cultures, needs to keep this image in mind. The cultural context for study resembles a mosaic of adjacent "neighborhoods" that define their individuality through their differences. This image may be more complex than a cultural text but it is also more realistic. What metaphor, then, might be more useful in expressing this reality than a linguistic text?

Tillich may be helpful. Tillich was also interested in reading cultural experiences as a theologian. To that end, he devised his method of correlation. His method "makes an analysis of the human situation out of which the existential questions arise, and it demonstrates that the symbols used in the Christian message are the answers to these questions" (Tillich 1951, vol. 1, 62). Tillich used a metaphor to visualize his method of correlation—a painting.[5] However, when Tillich offered his method of correlation as a way for theologians to approach the subject of culture, little did he have in mind the Latin American situation. Such a situation may be illustrated by the following anecdote.

I remember speaking to two different groups about the semiotics of culture. One group consisted of a homogenous sample of middle-class Anglo-Americans taking my master's degree class in theological anthropology. They were kind and wonderful students. Nonetheless, they had a certain degree of difficulty in grasping the concepts of signs and symbols, of boundaries and "meaning-space."

The other group consisted of a rather heterogenous group of brown Tex-Mex Chicanos, black Dominicans, white Cubans, and mestizo Peruvians. They also were a wonderful and marvelous group. They had come for a two-week workshop on the semiotics of culture. Many were ministers in the Roman Catholic Church, deacons, sisters, priests, and lay professionals. I was afraid that the semiotics of culture could not be taught in such a short time and dreaded the response when I first started talking about signs and boundaries. I was flabbergasted as they took the basic concepts of the semiotics of culture and began to make valid and relevant applications to their own work. I asked one of them whether he had learned the material before. He answered, "Hell, no! Professor Garcia, I live this stuff every day of my life!"

Many who live in the ambience of a dominant cultural group find their culture given to them on a silver platter. For them, culture is transparent. As they see it, it is the other—the member of the less-powerful minority culture—who has culture. Many who live in the ambience of a less-powerful cultural group, on the other hand, are quite aware of the culture of the more powerful dominant group. They become familiar with boundaries and binary oppositions.

The wisdom Hispanic-Americans bring to the specialist understanding of culture is that culture is not a bubble of meaning impervious to the world around it. The heterogeneity of my Hispanic-American class challenged the idea that culture somehow acts as a cookie-cutter that stamps out identical cultural beings. The painful experience of Hispanic-Americans is that one's culture is defined more by the violent and unequal encounter of cultures than by the culture itself. The insight of many Hispanic-Americans is that the experience of the violent and unequal encounter of cultures may be more fundamental than the experience of culture itself. We know we are cultural only because we perceive ourselves as different from another group. It is differences that make for the cultural experience.

The Hispanic-American reality is a bewildering variety of peoples, each with its separate history. The basic assumption behind Tillich's correlational theology is the encounter of the gospel with a single historical culture. Under the violent and unequal encounter of cultures, this basic assumption is transformed. No longer the correlation of gospel message with cultural situation, Tillich's method of correlation becomes the correlation of gospel messages present at the nexus of cultural encounters.

Tillich's visual metaphor—a painting—does not do justice to the violent and unequal encounter of cultures. In search for a new metaphor, one may consider Jorge Luis Borges' (1964, 23) description of Latin America as a "labyrinth of labyrinths." Borges' labyrinth is an apt metaphor for the violent and unequal encounter of cultures. A better metaphor for the Hispanic-American cultural context might be a composite metaphor of Tillich's painting and Borges' labyrinth—a mosaic.

A mosaic may be used as a metaphor intended to aid in visualizing the semiotics of culture in the Latin American and Hispanic-American cultural context. The violent and unequal encounter of cultures, in effect, may be visualized as creating a mosaic of "tiles." As such, a mosaic seems an excellent metaphor for the "little stories," each "little story" being represented by an individual tile which, in turn, can combine to form other "little stories." However, the metaphor of the mosaic has to be modified if the violent and unequal encounter of cultures is its referent. An ordinary mosaic is made up of permanently shaped tiles. A cultural mosaic, on the other hand, must allow the dynamics of cultural encounter to be represented. This means that the shape of the tiles of a cultural mosaic is not permanently fixed but may change according to the nature of the cultural encounter.

The semiotics of culture can be presented through the metaphor of a cultural mosaic of dynamic tiles emerging from the violent and unequal encounter of cultures. One can read such a mosaic from two pairs of perspectives.[6] One pair is known in the semiotics of culture as the inner and outer perspective. The inner perspective corresponds to an insider's perspective, that is, the perspective of the artist. Such a perspective attempts to read the mosaic as the artist would read it and corresponds to the perspective of a cultural insider. Most artists rarely want to interpret their work. They do, however, like to talk about it. The outer perspective, on the other hand, can be visualized as the perspective of an art critic and corresponds to a cultural outsider. Art critics, of course, interpret works of art such as a mosaic.[7]

Another pair of perspectives is known as the speaker and hearer perspective. The speaker-hearer perspective would correspond in our analogy to the artist-art critic perspective. Artists, for example, want their work displayed as is, without any additional embellishments. An artist would be horrified if anyone tried to change his or her work in any way. This concern corresponds to that of the cultural insider who wants his or her traditions communicated without changes. Art critics, on the other hand, simply want to understand and communicate the meaning of the artist's work. If they must do so by taking it apart, that does not represent a serious problem. The art critic represents an important perspective, the one of "hearer." The hearer corresponds to a cultural outsider who wants to understand the meaning of a cultural tradition, a tradition foreign to and not necessarily valued by him or her.[8]

Although there is a natural enmity between artists and art critics, they both need each other. The art critic gains wisdom by interpreting the work of the artist and communicates it to others. The artist, on the other hand, depends on the art critic to communicate the value of his or her work, so the work may continue uninterrupted. A fundamental problem takes place when art critics begin to speak of a work of art as if they were artists or artists begin to speak of their work as if they were art critics. A similar problem corresponds for specialists in the academy or Church and popular culture or religion. Often perspectives get mixed and both the insider and the outsider suffer as a result.[9]

This has led some to call for abandonment of any outsider perspectives. Only Hispanics can speak for other Hispanics, for example. This is misguided. The outsider perspective is vital to the insider. It protects the cultural insider from the demands and pressures of a more powerful outsider by providing understanding and communicating worth. The problem is the mixing of perspectives rather than their respective use. The semiotics of culture, by identifying and clarifying the issue of perspective, allows the specialist to continue interpreting the works of others with confidence. What the semiotics of culture demands is that the specialist be clear about what perspective to use and then use it consistently. The perspective to be used here in reading the "little stories" of St. Martín de Porres is a thoroughly outsider perspective, an outer-hearer perspective. This work is intended to communicate the value of the "little stories" and make them understandable to those who may not be familiar with them.[10] I am aware that the popular tradition of St. Martín de Porres is not the property of Hispanic-American Catholics. Many Catholics and non-Catholics claim St. Martín de Porres as part of their tradition. If I am to be faulted in this work, let it be because I did not keep this perspective in mind, not because I have chosen to use it.

The metaphor of a cultural mosaic highlights two important principles at work in the violent and unequal encounter of cultures: identity and change.[11] Focusing on these two principles frees one from having to choose one model of culture among the hundreds that exist. All we need take into account are the twin principles of cultural encounter—identity and change. These two principles correspond in the metaphor of a cultural mosaic to the tile and the grout lines that make up its boundaries.

Identity in the mosaic metaphor corresponds to a tile. Each tile is, in essence, a unit of identity. The shape, color, and shading of each tile not only give identity to the tile but give meaning and nuance to the mosaic as a whole. The grout lines, or boundaries of each tile, correspond to the principle of change. Any little shift in those grout lines or boundaries changes the shape and identity of a tile. In a cultural mosaic, these boundaries are capable of changing. Thus, a cultural mosaic has structure as well as dynamics, each corresponding to the principles of identity and cultural change, respectively, the *sine qua non* of the violent and unequal encounter of cultures.

THE SEMIOSPHERE

Each "little story" in the beatification process of St. Martín de Porres corresponds to a tile and its borders. The set of "little stories" form the cultural text which, in this metaphor, becomes a cultural mosaic consisting of tiles, each carrying information about identity and change. Tiles also help visualize an important concept in the semiotics of culture, the *semiosphere*.[12] A semiosphere is akin to a biosphere.[13] A biosphere contains within it all the necessary processes and elements for a particular way of life to exist. A semiosphere contains within it all the necessary signs, codes, and messages for a way of life to be expressed. A tile is a way of visualizing the semiosphere. Biospheres, however, may contain within themselves smaller biospheres. The biosphere of a pond may include the biosphere of a lily pad. Semiospheres, similarly, contain within themselves smaller semiospheres. These are known in the semiotics of culture as *semiotic domains*. Both semiospheres and semiotic domains contain the means by which concepts can be communicated. A semiosphere, for example, may contain within it a "vegetable" semiotic domain and a "cooking" semiotic domain, which allows a recipe for vegetable soufflé to be communicated to someone within the same semiosphere.

Just as biospheres can be given a name (tidal pool, prairie, etc.) so can semiospheres and semiotic domains. This takes place through metaphors.[14] Metaphors consist of an intricate web of interlocked signs and codes that suggest the nature of the signs and codes of the semiotic space they name. The metaphor of "healing" conjures up a complex of meanings and messages that give an idea of what healing refers to. Metaphors, however, can also be compared to one another.[15] St. Martín, for example, appears as happy as a "dove." Such comparisons are a mapping of one semiotic domain, the "St. Martín" domain, to another, the dove domain. Such comparisons help one understand what the St. Martín domain contains. When such comparisons, however, are unusual, more than understanding is taking place. When St. Martín treats animals as if they were human, the "human" domain is not only being compared to the "animal" domain but also transformed by it. Thus, metaphors are important clues to the structure of a cultural mosaic.

SEMIOTIC BOUNDARIES

All semiospheres and semiotic domains have one thing in common: they all possess boundaries. Two adjacent tiled spaces possess a common boundary. The boundary, then, is not so much a category as it is a relationship.[16] The boundary between a "cat" domain or tile and a "mouse" domain or tile, for example, can be represented by the relationship "eat"/"be eaten." The boundary between these two tiled spaces is known as a *semiotic boundary* and is usually indicated by a relationship consisting of a pair of opposites. A semiotic boundary indicates the dynamics of a cultural mosaic, the ability of a cultural mosaic to adjust to changes in the nature of the cultural encounters.

Semiotic boundaries are the front lines of cultural change. When a cultural mosaic is about to change shape, great activity of the signs[17] and codes near a boundary takes place. St. Martín, for example, fights with demons.[18] Thus miracles may be seen as, for example, the crossing of a boundary between two worlds—the world of the everyday and the world of the sacred. A miracle that occurs regularly in the "little stories" is bilocation. Bilocation, being in two places at the same time, is an example of a code reversal. A normal code concerning location in space would rule that you cannot be in two places at once. Bilocation reverses this code. Code reversal is a symptom of high semiotic activity. St. Martín also speaks to mice and dogs, and a dog, cat, and mouse drink peacefully at his feet from the same bowl of soup. This kind of semiotic activity indicates the presence of semiotic boundaries, and one of the most satisfying techniques of the semiotics of culture is their identification.

Semiotic boundaries are indicated by the presence of *binary opposition*. Binary opposition takes the form of stark contrasts: left versus right, up versus down. When St. Martín, for example, brings dogs in to his cell when all the other friars tell him they should be out of the convent, a binary opposition is at work. A way to visualize binary opposition is as the opposition of spaces across a semiotic boundary. Thus finding examples of binary opposition is another technique for discovering the underlying structure of a cultural mosaic.[19] Binary oppositions, however, may be related to one another and thus transformed. Such an operation is known as *binary parallelism* and may be visualized as connecting two separate grout lines of a mosaic by a third so as to make a new grout line, that is to say, changing the look of a mosaic and, thus, its meaning.

STEPS IN THE SEMIOTICS OF CULTURE

The above concepts—perspective, semiosphere, semiotic boundary, and binary opposition—are essential for a semiotics of culture. The semiotics of culture provides a method by which to recognize the "Big Story" in the "little stories" making up a cultural mosaic. The aim of this work is to "read" the "little stories" of St. Martín de Porres using this method. The semiotics of culture has been discussed, but its method has remained merely a suggestion. It is possible, however, to provide a schema for the method of the semiotics of culture. Such a schema would consist of three parts: perspective, structure, and dynamics.

Part I: Perspective

(1) Pick a perspective. This step is another way to say: choose your audience. Once the audience is chosen, remain consistent and do not mix perspectives. The possibilities of perspective are, essentially, four. One can pick from either an inner-speaker, inner-hearer, outer-hearer, or outer-speaker perspective. These have been discussed in a previous chapter. As mentioned previously, the perspective chosen in this work is the outer-hearer perspective.

Part II: Structure

(2) Locate a cultural mosaic. This, of course, is a crucial step. Finding a cultural mosaic is easier said than done. Previous discussion, I hope, has convinced the reader that many cultural mosaics may be found in popular religion.

(3) Make an inventory of the mosaic's major signs. Having located the cultural mosaic, what are its obvious and not-so-obvious signs? Are these signs common to all cultural groups involved?

(4) Identify recurrent metaphors. Metaphors that recur again and again obviously name important semiotic domains. The major goal of this important step, however, is to identify the root metaphor.

(5) Identify recurrent binary oppositions. Such binary oppositions signal the presence of semiotic boundaries. The location of the semiotic boundaries is crucial not only in mapping the structure of the cultural mosaic but also in understanding its dynamics.

(6) Identify the codes at work in the cultural mosaic. How are things done? This is the basic question that guides the search for codes. Do people normally lay down in bed when sick? What do people do with sick animals? The answers to such questions reveal the codes of a cultural mosaic. Like semiotic boundaries, codes not only aid in discerning the structure of a cultural mosaic but also its dynamics. For example, do people walk through doors? Do animals speak? These are examples of codes being reversed.

Part III: Dynamics of the Cultural "Mosaic"

(7) Identify metaphorical mapping. Are certain metaphors being compared or used together in a simile that is unusual? Are animals being treated as if they were people? Finding these mappings provides a clue as to the dynamics of a cultural mosaic—the transformations of meaning taking place.

(8) Identify binary parallelisms. Are binary oppositions being compared? Are certain binary oppositions being reversed? Do the mighty now bow down and are the lowly raised high? When these occur in triads, the middle term reveals the shifting of a semiotic boundary and the creation of a new semiotic domain.

(9) Finally, consider the sociohistorical dimension. What signs point to the history of the cultural mosaic? Are there signs that correspond to some other time or to a continuation into the present of another time? In the case of Lima, for example, are there signs that deal with sickness, signs that may point to the great epidemics of smallpox? Are there signs that may have their source in the slaving ships of another century—mice, for example? The dynamics of a cultural mosaic depends in great part on its sociohistorical

dimension. Thus, it is crucial to examine a cultural mosaic for the signs that reveal its history.

The above provides a schema that corresponds to the method of semiotics of culture followed in this work. Although the schema is presented as a sequence, the actual analysis need not follow the sequence in strict order. Obviously, one needs to locate a cultural mosaic before proceeding to find the codes of the mosaic. On the other hand, one could start by noticing recurrent metaphors in some cultural phenomena, which may aid in identifying a cultural mosaic. In the final analysis, the semiotics of culture, as presented in this work, is more an art than a science. Nonetheless, it is also a powerful method which opens up the richness and profundity of the "little stories."

THE SOCIOHISTORICAL ELEMENT
IN THE SEMIOTICS OF CULTURE

As Elizondo suggested in his method, the "little stories" contain both a symbolic-cultural and a sociohistorical dimension. These two together provide the reader of "little stories" with the tools needed to reveal the "Big Story" being told. At first glance, the semiotics of culture seems rather unfriendly to any historical analysis. Messages, after all, take place in real time, the time of the eternal present, ahistorical time. Or do they?

The insight coming from the experience of a violent and unequal encounter of cultures is that signs and symbols have a history, a social history of encounter and conflict, and that this history may itself be a sign. Semiotic boundaries and semiospheres also exist across time. Thus, a semiotics of culture ought also to look for these special signs and semiotic domains, signs which point across time and space to the meaning of the present and semiotic domains which provide continuity of signs, codes, and messages between past, present, and future. The semiotics of culture, then, is not complete without an analysis of the sociohistorical dimension of the cultural mosaic. This is the subject of the next chapter.

4

The Violent and Unequal
Encounter of Cultures

A question I often place before students asks what brought the notion of culture to their attention. Most students become aware of culture through an unexpected conflict with someone or some group of another culture. Such encounters are well known to many Hispanic-Americans, indeed, to any minority living in a more powerful dominant culture. To those in the dominant culture, however, culture is transparent. It is the minority that has culture. Culture apparently only becomes visible in the unequal encounter with another culture. In fact, many Hispanic-Americans are asking whether the violent and unequal encounter between cultures is a more fundamental reality than culture itself.

This question of Hispanic-Americans has been given its deepest explora-tion by Virgilio Elizondo. Elizondo was the first to name the significance of the violent and unequal encounter of cultures: *Mestizaje*. Mestizaje refers to the process of biological and cultural mixing that occurs after the violent and unequal encounter between cultures. Such mixing also creates frontiers. The meaning of the frontiers caused by the violent and unequal encounter of cultures poses a special significance for Elizondo (1988, x):

I often ask myself the question: Is the frontier between the United States and Mexico the border between two nations or is it the frontier zone of a new human race? . . . The border between the United States and Mexico has been described by Octavio Paz, the great philosopher of Mexico, as the border between absolute otherness. It is not just the border between two countries, but the border between two humanities: between two worlds, two periods of time, two historical processes, two languages, two drastically different ways of life, two core cultural ideologies. The 3500 kilometers between the two countries is the political border between two nations, but it is much more. It is the meeting point and often the site of violent clash between two radically different civilizations . . . In the Southwest of the United States, the North of planet earth is meeting the South, and the result transcends old barriers by fusing North and South into a new synthesis. In this portion of the earth, differences are not destroyed, hidden, or ignored; they are absorbed to become the active ingredients of a new human group. The borders no longer mark the end limits of a country, a civilization, or even a hemisphere, but the starting points of a new space populated by a new human group. To be an intimate part of the birth of this nueva raza is indeed a fascinating experience.

The significance of the violent and unequal encounter of cultures for Elizondo lies in a human process more fundamental than culture itself, the creation of many-culture, the Mestizaje of the human being, a new creation toward a new and exciting future humanity.

The semiotics of culture, happily, is quite at home with boundaries or frontiers. When applied to the reality of the violent and unequal encounter of cultures, the semiotics of culture becomes more than the analysis of culture. From a Hispanic-American perspective, the semiotics of culture becomes not so much the study of culture *per se* but the study of a more fundamental reality, the boundaries or frontiers created by the violent and unequal encounter of cultures, the many-culture of Mestizaje.

The reality of the violent and unequal encounter of cultures also adds an important dimension to the semiotics of culture. If the violent and unequal encounter of cultures is a more fundamental reality than culture itself, then the signs of a culture have a history. Signs in the violent and unequal encounter of cultures also point to a past—a past responsible for the present. By pointing to the past, the history of a sign becomes a sign as well. The semiotics of culture also can determine the history of a sign of a particular cultural mosaic since such a history is, in essence, a sign as well. The semiotics of culture, in fact, is capable of identifying the particular sociohistorical currents responsible for the cultural mosaic under study. As such, the semiotics of culture acknowledges that there exist cultural messages across time, messages carried by the history of a sign which is a sign in itself.

The above discussion relates to the pioneer work of Elizondo in reading the "little story." Elizondo demonstrated the fecundity of both a symbolic-cultural and a sociohistorical approach when applied to a popular cultural mosaic. With the added understanding of the fundamental reality of the violent and unequal encounter of cultures, the semiotics of culture becomes a formal method through which Elizondo's insights can be applied. The semiotics of culture, with the added understanding mentioned above, will make sure that the "little stories" of St. Martín de Porres will be read not only with the symbolic-cultural dimension in mind but also with the socio-historical dimension that took part in their creation. The following describes the violent and unequal encounters between Iberian, sub-Saharan, and Native American cultures which provide the sociohistorical dimension necessary for the application of the semiotics of culture to St. Martín's cultural mosaic.

THE ENCOUNTER WITH NATIVE AMERICA

In the presence of 168 conquistadores, Francisco Pizarro executed the Inca King Atahualpa by garroting in 1533 (Cobo 1979, 171). In doing so, Pizarro declared a new empire and sealed it by the founding of *Ciudad de los Tres Reyes* on January 5, 1535. The name of this new city did not survive history. The Spanish name *Ciudad de los Tres Reyes* was supplanted by the Quechuan name, Lima.[1] Thus began one of the many violent and unequal encounters between Iberian and Native American cultures which, in its wake, left many puzzles.

One of the great puzzles in this history is the relative ease with which the conquistadores conquered the indigenous. Alfred Crosby believes that European diseases are to blame for this mass extermination. He observed that few of the killer diseases were native to America. The Amerindian, he claims, simply had no defenses for the diseases brought over from other continents. He quotes a German missionary who said in 1699 that "the Indians die so easily that the bare look and smell of a Spaniard causes them to give up the ghost" (Crosby 1972, 37).[2] Borah and Cook believe that in less than a century after contact with Europeans, only 4 percent of the preconquest population of Mexico remained.[3] The epidemics involved in the depopulation included smallpox (*bubas*), hemorrhagic smallpox (*sarampion viruelas*), typhus (*peste*), influenza, measles, mumps, diphtheria, and scarlet fever (Dobyns 1963, 493-515).

The ravages of disease among the Incas of Peru had tragic consequences for the people of Africa. The connecting link was the rich silver and gold mines in the Andes, mines such as the silver mine at Potosí. The mine at Potosí was discovered in 1545 by the Inca Huallpa, who, trying to recover a runaway llama, had to spend the night in the highlands. At 14,000 feet, Huallpa built a fire to ward off the cold. In the reflection of the flames, he noticed the glint of a long silver vein in the side of the mountain. This streak of silver revealed a huge store of silver.[4] The silver of the Andes of Peru not only affected the indigenous and the African but also the European.[5] Charles V bestowed on Potosí the title of Imperial city with the inscription: "I am rich Potosí, treasurer of the world, king of the mountains, envy of kings" (Galeano 1973, 32).

THE ENCOUNTER WITH SUB-SAHARAN AFRICA

The demographic collapse of the indigenous population, along with the need to work the silver mines of Potosí, led to an increase in the Atlantic slave trade.[6] Very early in the sixteenth century, the Spaniards were confronted with a rapidly diminishing Indian labor force. The black slaves available—those born in Iberia (*ladinos*)—were too few in number. Soon a clamor arose to import slaves directly from Africa (*bozales*). The Spanish Crown heard the clamor, and the transatlantic slave trade was underway (Kiple 1987, 7).[7]

The slave trade, however, also imported unwanted cargoes. The West Africans, like the Europeans before them, carried deadly diseases to the New World. Among them were falciparum malaria and yellow fever. These ferocious killers fell on the Europeans just as the European disease of smallpox had fallen on the Indians (Kiple 1987, 8).

Most of the slaves originated in the West African coast, specifically from the section known as the Ríos de Guinea between the Senegal and Niger rivers. By the late sixteenth century, the Congo-Angola section would be exploited for its human capital (Bowser 1974, 44). The first port the slave traders saw after leaving Africa was Cartagena. Lima, however, became an important slaving port as Peru's need for slave labor increased. By the sixteenth century, the Peruvian slave commerce increased between Panama and Callao, the port of Lima (Bowser 1974, 54, 55). This commercial slave triangle of Cartagena-Panama-Lima (Callao) brought a great influx of Africans to the New World. Estimates of the total number of African slaves delivered to the Spanish Indies ranges from 1 to 5 million (Rout 1976, 64). In fact, it is estimated that the number of slaves in Lima grew from 4,000 in 1586 to some 7,000 in the 1590s to some 20,000 by 1640, so by the last decade of the sixteenth century, Lima was half black and would stay that way for most of the seventeeth century (Klein 1986, 33).

THE GREAT MESTIZAJE

As the mix of Europeans, indigenous, and Africans increased in Latin America, a new context was developing: the beginnings of the great biological mix of populations, the Mestizaje, which is the concern of Elizondo. We have a witness to this great Mestizaje in the writings of Garcilaso de la Vega (1539-1612), a mestizo himself (1966, 607-8):

> We were forgetting the best imports into the Indies, namely the Spaniards, and the Negroes who have since been taken there as slaves, for they were previously unknown in my country. These two races have mingled [with the Indians] in various ways to form others which are

distinguished by the use of different names. Although I spoke a little about this in the *History of Florida,* I have decided to repeat it here, as being the proper place. Thus any Spanish man or woman who arrives from Spain is called a Spaniard or Castilian, the two words being quite interchangeable in Peru; and I have used them indifferently in this history and in the *Florida.* The children of Spaniards by Spanish women born there are called *criollos* or *criollas,* implying that they were born in the Indies. The name was invented by the Negroes, as its use shows. They use it to mean a Negro born in the Indies, and they devised it to distinguish those who come from this side and were born in Guinea from those born in the New World, since the former are held in greater honor and considered to be of higher rank because they were born in a strange land. The parents take offence if they are called *criollos.* The Spaniards have copied them in this way. Both Spaniards and Guinea Negroes are called *criollos* if they are born in the New World. The Negro who arrives there from the Old World is called Negro or Guineo. The child of a Negro by an Indian woman or of an Indian and a Negro woman is called *mulato* or *mulata.* Their children are called *cholos,* a word from the Windward Island: it means a dog but it is not used for a thoroughbred dog, but only for a mongrel cur: the Spaniards use the word in a pejorative and vituperative sense. The children of Spaniards by Indians are called *mestizos,* meaning that we are a mixture of the two races. The word was applied by the first Spaniards who had children by Indian women, and because it was used by our fathers, as well as on account of its meaning, I call myself by it in public and am proud of it, though in the Indies, if a person is told: You're a Mestizo or He's a Mestizo it is taken as an insult.

This great mixture profoundly affected the nature of Latin American civilization. The great Mestizaje witnessed by Garcilaso de la Vega gave an unparalleled "social polychromy" (Crespo 1964, 60). The color of the skin reflected the hierarchization of the society, although it was not the definitive cause. Other factors such as the pedigree of parents and the size of one's wealth made the picture of colonial society more complex. The worst situation, however, existed for those of mixed race. The mestizos "were considered diminished or incapable of certain tasks, or public charges, of becoming priests, or even to study in the University" (Crespo 1964, 60-61).

Indeed, colonial Spanish American society was divided between the Hispanic *gente de razón* (people with reason) and the non-Hispanic others (Hoberman and Socolow 1986, 7). [8] The strong emphasis given to reason can be seen in the high priority given to the speedy establishment of universities. St. Mark, the first university to be founded in the Americas, was founded with astonishing speed in 1551 by the Dominicans, St. Martín's order.[9] There was good reason for this. The conquest of the New World raised profound questions about the world and about the human being, questions begun in the political exercise of conquest and spilling over into the university hall of the theologian.

THE VALLADOLID DEBATE

The political questions raised by the conquest of America ended up in the theologian's lap. It is a remarkable event in western intellectual tradition. As Hanke put it (1959, ix):

One of the most curious episodes in the intellectual history of the Western world occurred when two remarkable Spaniards—Bartolomé de las Casas and Juan Ginés de Sepúlveda—met in Valladolid in 1550 to debate this issue. Then for the first, and doubtless for the last, time a colonizing nation organized a formal enquiry into the justice of the methods used to extend its empire.

The impetus for this debate was the institution called *Encomienda.*

THE ENCOMIENDA

The Encomienda, in the eyes of the Iberian colonists, was a quasi-contract with the Amerindian in which tribute of labor is exchanged for education in the Christian faith and accommodation of physical needs. It originated with the 1493 papal bulls of donation—(*Inter Caetera* (May 3-4) and *Dudum Siquidem* (September 23)—which "donate," "grant," and "assign" the new and yet-to-be-found lands. With the donation came the exclusive responsibility of the Catholic monarchs and descendants for converting the native inhabitants to the Christian faith.[10]

The first reference to the Encomienda is given in 1503 in a royal decree that apportioned the Amerindians to different communities so they might be managed in a more efficacious way.[11] This apportionment (*repartimiento*) was coined the Encomienda by King Fernando with a decree given August 14, 1509, to Diego Colón, admiral and governor of the Indies, in order to clarify what regulations with the indigenous ought to be (Rivera-Pagn 1991, 195). The Encomienda was rooted in the entrenched belief that true human beings were beings who by nature made laws and built cities. The initial (but mistaken) observation that the Caribbean Indians possessed no laws or cities signaled an anthropological challenge to the Iberians.

The belief that man is a natural city-maker and lawmaker has its source in Aristotle. The *Politics* defines man as an animal who naturally communicates with speech or "logos," and as an animal who makes laws and cities (*polis*).[12] A wood engraving of 1505, one of the earliest descriptions of the Amerindian, had the following inscription (Eames 1922, 759):

> They go naked, both men and women; they have well-shaped bodies, and in colour nearly red; they bore holes in their cheeks, lips, noses and ears, and stuff these holes with blue stones, crystals, marble and alabaster, very fine and beautiful. This custom is followed alone by the men. They have no personal property, but all things are in common. They all live together without a king and without a government, and every one is his own master. They take for wives whom they first meet, and in all this they have no rule. They also war with each other, and without art or rule. And they eat one another, and those they slay are eaten, for human flesh is a common food. In the houses salted human flesh is hung up to dry. They live to be a hundred and fifty years old, and are seldom sick.

The Encomienda seemed plausible in light of these city-less and lawless Caribbean Indians. It is little wonder, then, that the Crown felt Amerindians had to be "rescued" from their own ignorance and animallike habits by "commending" them into the hands of the "civilized."

Yet the Encomienda was a strange institution. The *encomendado* was technically a free man. He did not belong to his master and could not, by law, be sold or exchanged for another Indian. These distinctions, however, were not made in practice. Encomendados, in practice, were rarely given any education, nor were their physical needs accommodated, as the demographic collapse well attests. When the missionary orders followed the colonists, the focus of their protests was the legitimacy of this institution.[13]

In 1519, the violent and unequal encounter of Cortez with Mexico brought the issue of the Encomienda to the steps of the Crown. The encounter with the Aztecs showed them to have cities and laws, unlike the Caribbean Indians. This "discovery" of the "advanced" Indian pressed the anthropological challenge.[14] The Caribbean Indian could be classified as a barbarian like the Tartars and the Germanic tribes. The challenge of the advanced Indian, however, was not so easily overcome. The advanced Indian built cities like civilized human beings yet committed barbaric acts such as cannibalism, and human sacrifice. The advanced Indian presented human difference in such a way that the Spanish Crown could no longer ignore the anthropological challenge: Are human beings universally alike? Or can human beings be truly different from one another? The medieval category was the other, a different human being. A different human being, however, is not the same as a human being that is different. The medieval category of the other fell short of such distinctions. These questions could only be answered through new human categories.

The medieval category of the other, a different human being, was the pagan. Pagans, in turn, were divided into three broad categories: (1) *de iure*, those who live outside the Church but on lands once part of the Roman empire and thus part of the *dominium* of the Church, (2) *de facto*, those living anywhere in the world, yet lawfully subject to a Christian ruler, and (3) those who dwell in lands which are neither under legitimate Christian rule nor living within the bounds of the Roman world. These are the *infideles* who are neither de iure, nor de facto (Cajetan 1888-1906, 94). This last category, however, was divided into two other categories according to the nature of their paganism: those who, in Aquinas' words, were "invincibly ignorant," who had never heard the gospel, and those who were "vincibly ignorant," who had refused the gospel, folks such as Jews and Muslims (Aquinas 1975, Ia IIae, q.10, art.1).

It soon became evident that the Amerindian only fit one category: the invincibly ignorant. The Alexandrian bulls and the Encomienda, in light of the advanced Indian, had set up a political conundrum: by what rights had the Crown of Castile taken possession of land unknown before in history? Moreover, how could the inhabitants of these new lands be both vassals and slaves of the Crown at the same time? (Padgen 1986, 36). The Valladolid debate started out as a search for a legal answer to this question. Such an answer, however, proved to be impossible. The question could only be answered anthropologically. The debate, in essence, was a search for a new category of human being.

THE THREE PERSPECTIVES OF THE VALLADOLID DEBATE

The encounter with the advanced Indians, the Aztec and Inca, led to a search for new categories of human being. This search was spearheaded by three well-defined perspectives that can be demonstrated from a survey of the literature on Aztec themes between 1530 and 1600 (Keen 1990, 77-78). The majority of writers were obviously hostile to the Aztec and Indians, in general. This group, closely tied to the interests of the encomendero, counted among them Francisco López de Gómara, Gonzalo Fernández de Oviedo, and Juan Ginés de Sepúlveda. A second, smaller group of writers adamantly opposed the Encomienda and slavery of the Indians. They generally held a positive and exalted view of the Indians. Their defense of the Amerindian rested on the universality of humanity, the Amerindian being "like us." Bartolomé de las Casas is, perhaps, the most famous representative of this group.

The next group of writers held a shaky and uncertain middle ground. These were pragmatist clergy who had little patience for farfetched or intricate rationalizations such as those of Las Casas. Their position was the most realistic of the three. Equivocally, they saw the Encomienda as beneficial, yet they abhorred the excesses and abuse of the Indians by the encomenderos. Their equivocation stemmed from a true grasp of the anthropological challenge. This group correctly perceived that they were dealing with neither an animal nor an unqualified universal humanity but with human beings with true differences. Many consider this group to be the developers of the great ethnographic tradition that is used today by cultural anthropologists (*see* Smith 1985, Burridge 1991, McGrane 1989). Unfortunately, this group described the nature of these human differences in terms that played right into the hands of the encomenderos. This group included Motolinía, Bernardino de Sagahún, and Francisco de Vitoria.

The first perspective—outright hostility—presented itself at Valladolid in the form of Sepúlveda. The second perspective—exalted praise for the Amerindian—made its presence known through Bartolomé de las Casas. As such, these points of view were flip sides of the same coin. This coin was the true difference presented by the Amerindian, a difference which could not be dismissed either by denying the Amerindian their humanity (Sepúlveda) or their difference (Las Casas). These positions represented a certain confusion about the nature of the challenge presented by the Amerindians, human beings with true differences. The moderate position came closer to understanding the real issue. Vitoria, I believe, grasped the anthropological challenge of true human difference presented by the Amerindian, even though he failed to describe it. The failure was tragic. Vitoria's perspective transformed empire building from a pursuit based on cross and sword (Catholics against infidels) to one based on culture (superior Spaniard against inferior people).

SEPÚLVEDA: THE MAJORITY PERSPECTIVE

In 1548, three of Vitoria's best pupils, Melchor Cano, Bartolomé de Carranza, and Diego de Covarrubias, were called in to examine a work by the emperor's chaplain and official chronicler, Juan Ginés de Sepúlveda, a work called *Democrates secundus*.[15] Sepúlveda, an Italian, skillfully translated Aristotle.[16] Sepúlveda, however, thought in rigidly orthodox and chauvinistic terms. *Democrates secundus* presented the majority perspective on the Amerindian and consisted of a dialogue between Democrates and the Lutheran Leopoldo.[17] Sepúlveda relied heavily on a previous argument used by the Scottish theologian John Mair. Mair argued that Aristotle's natural slave, a being possessing a mind but not in control of it, could be applied as a category to describe the new barbarians, the Amerindians.[18] Mair argued that the hierarchy of being that informed both Christians and Greeks was not constructed in sharp divisions. Between categories there existed a region where categories became mixed in what Aquinas called the "connexio rerum" (1975, 1.68). Thus between the categories of animal and human there existed a region where both categories mixed. There a being could exist that was part human, part animal—Aristotle's natural slave (Padgen 1986, 22).

Sepúlveda found the category he was looking for in the thought of John Mair. This category Sepúlveda called *homunculi*,[19] little men with little trace of humanity. According to Sepúlveda, true men possessed genuine humanity and were moral, intelligent, free persons who are, by definition, Spaniards. The Amerindian, on the other hand, was immoral in his cannibalism and human sacrifice. The Amerindian was, in fact, "more like monkeys than men" (Sepúlveda 1892, 305).

Sepúlveda would have solved the Crown's legal and political conundrum by claiming that the Amerindian was subhuman, a homunculus. Sepúlveda used an anthropological argument rather than a legal one—the Amerindians were somewhere in between human and animal. Such an argument, however, failed to rise to the radical anthropological challenge that the Amerindian raised. Sepúlveda's anthropology was, in essence, a dismissal of the anthropological question, for if the Amerindian were not human, the issues of just war or rightful conquest did not apply. Indeed, the Spanish had a duty to make war against such homunculi for they committed crimes against nature (Sepúlveda 1892, 309). Las Casas, in a sense, did no better.

LAS CASAS: THE MINORITY PERSPECTIVE

While Sepúlveda denigrated the humanity of the Amerindian, Las Casas exalted it (de las Casas 1988, 105):

> They are not ignorant, inhuman or bestial, but before having heard the word "Spaniard," they had estates rightly organized, that is, prudently administered with excellent laws, religion and institutions. They cultivated friendships and, united in a living society, inhabited large cities, in which they prudently, with justice and equity, administered the business not only of peace but also of war, governed by laws such that, in many aspects, are superior to ours and could cause admiration in the wise men of Athens.

Las Casas put forth his argument using the same strategy as Sepúlveda, searching for a new category to describe the Amerindian. Las Casas began his *Apologiae* by demonstrating similarity between widely separated cultural groups. As such, Las Casas, like Sepúlveda, recognized difference in the Amerindian, but this difference was not "real." According to Las Casas, the Amerindian difference was due to an upbringing, a social condition. In essence, the Amerindian was human. Indeed, all nations are human. The differences observed were not fundamental.

Las Casas set out his argument in the *Apologiae* with broad but thorough essays on aspects of ancient cultures from over 370 ancient sources, comparing them with similar aspects of the Amerindian. Las Casas' motive was to dismantle the reading of "natural slave" in Aristotle's *Politics*. Las Casas' major thesis in the book claimed that Aristotle gave the name "barbarians" to two different cultural types. Las Casas, however, discerned four.

The first type was comprised of those whose minds have been over-whelmed by their passions and are full of the sin of *ferocitas* (de las Casas 1988, 1.14). The second and third types depended on the Thomistic distinc-tion between *simpliciter* and *secundum quid* as they apply to language (de las Casas 1988, 2.15-22). Simpliciter referred to something that had no qualification. Secundum quid, on the other hand, was something qualified by something else. Thus, if the word *barbarian* were to connote "strangeness or foreignness," this barbarism would be purely relative. He belongs with the other but is human all the same. If, on the other hand, a subject is strange to the human race as a whole, then his barbarism is precisely the feature that distinguishes him without further qualification. This is characterized by a state of linguistic anarchy in which men do not know their own speech.

There is, however, a further dimension to the linguistic distinction be-tween barbarian and civilized: written language. Without written knowledge, each generation has to discover anew the cultural knowledge it requires to improve itself. Thus Las Casas makes two more categories: barbarians secundum quid having no written language, primitive but not fundamentally barbaric, and barbarians simpliciter, the "natural slaves," the fundamental barbarian. These latter, however, were rare and anomalous (de las Casas 1988, 2.17). The fourth category of barbarian is the non-Christian (de las Casas 1988, 5.28-30v.). Without access to mysteries of the Christian faith, non-Christians commit crimes against nature. In sum, Las Casas placed the Indians under both the fourth category, as pagans, and the second, barbarians secundum quid. This meant that the barbarism perceived in the Amerindian was relative, not essential.

Las Casas then came up with his own categories to argue that the Amerindian's difference was relative, not essential. As such, Las Casas' perspective dismisses radical difference. The Amerindian is essentially like us. True human difference is not real but relative. Under the banner of one universal humanity, Las Casas took the opposite perspective from Sepúlveda. The Valladolid debate turned on anthropological categories, but it failed to rise to the anthropological challenge posed by the Americas. One perspective dismissed the challenge by revitalizing an ancient category (the natural slave), the other by modifying obscure ones (the barbarian secundum quid). However, it was the third perspective, I believe, that truly grasped the notion of real human difference, even while it failed to come to terms with it.

VITORIA: THE MODERATE PERSPECTIVE

The Salamanca School developed between 1520 and 1530 at the Univer-sity of Salamanca.[20] The Dominican Francisco de Vitoria wanted to revital-ize scholastic theology by including ethical dilemmas that come up in everyday life. Vitoria, in a sense, wanted to revitalize narrow, scholastic concerns through a specialized rather than a specialist focus. Vitoria believed that "inescapable conclusions of the rational mind" could be based on self-evident first principles inherent in *ius naturae* or natural law. The concept of nature that guided Sepúlveda's and Vitoria's theology had its formative origins in the twelfth century. M. D. Chenu describes the period as featuring "an essentially religious discovery of the universe through a discovery of Nature" (1968, 48).

The discovery of Nature was essentially the realization that the human confronted an "external, present, intelligible, and active reality" within which the human was also caught up within such Nature. Indeed, humans were "themselves bits of this comos" (Chenu 1968, 5). Such realization was developed and articulated by William of Conches and the Chartres theologians. The discovery of Nature brought with it the perception of the universe as an "admirably ordered unity."

Such unity demanded a continuity that found its greatest tension at the problem of integrating human nature into such a unified universe. Human nature was, after all, the meeting point of matter and intelligence, sense and spirit, *imago mundi* and *imago Dei*. This human compositum, this cosmic Mestizaje, represented the immense unity of all things by standing at the "paradoxical borderline" between matter and spirit. The world-soul of the Timaeus and the hierarchical principle of Pseudo-Dyonisius were brought together to resolve this tension in the thirteenth century. A progressive, ordered chain of all beings was the result. Such a chain brought causality and meaning together and allowed Vitoria to formulate his influential theology of natural precepts.

Natural law, according to Vitoria, was the efficient cause behind society's practice. As such, it provided the ground for entering areas of ethical concerns that had remained unexplored. Vitoria's Salamanca School assumed people by their very nature possessed the capacity to know good from evil through *prima praecepta* or "first principles" given them by God in Creation.[21] These first principles, however, are not what we see in human behavior. They are the primary cause. What we see are secondary causes, and these form the basis for society's laws. A theologian, in cases where the law observed is in question or little understood, can presumably begin with abstract first principles to illumine or challenge the law in question (Padgen 1986, 61). This theory of natural law provided Vitoria with the framework in which he placed the problem caused by the institution of the Encomienda.

Iberian theologians usually were solicited by the Crown to work on a specified problem. This they did in conjunction with the Crown's jurists and administrative officials in the confines of a *junta,* an official meeting where opinions and reflections were given. The resulting documents were then collected and recommendations were given to the Crown. Vitoria's school of theologians, on the other hand, worked independently of the Crown. The opinions of Vitoria and his Salamanca School were expressed not in the confines of the junta, but in the lecture hall. They aimed toward explanation and solution rather than a legal ruling.

The unsolicited reflections of the Salamanca School on the nature of the Amerindian were provoked by news of the cruelty of the Encomienda system abroad. Francisco de Vitoria was angered by news of Francisco Pizarro's 1534 execution of the Inca Atahualpa.[22] His reflections on the Amerindian in his "relectio De indis," his lecture notes of 1539, impacted every subsequent discussion on the Indies. "De indis" set out to find a solution to a problem—what were the just titles for the conquest of America?

Vitoria felt that the typical jurist approach to the challenge of the Encomienda had failed because it was a new and unprecedented situation.[23] As such, Vitoria had turned the nature of the practice of the Encomienda from a political problem over the legitimacy of the Alexandrian bulls to a profound anthropological question. By making the affair of the Indies something more than the territorial rights of pagans and a matter for the *lex divina,* or natural law, then "it became, by definition, a matter touching on the very nature of man (anthropology) and the metaphysics of the social order" (Padgen 1986, 67). Vitoria had identified the true issue. It was not simply a new land that had been discovered but also a new humanity.

Vitoria set out his argument for a new anthropology by examining the legal titles by which the Crown could possibly justify the Encomienda and systematically invalidating each of them. The first possible title was based on Augustine's conclusion that denial of right of passage constitutes an injury sufficient for war. Augustine based this conclusion on the biblical account of the Israelite's attack on the Amorites (Num. 21:21-5) (Augustine 1954, 4.44). The Iberians could legally wage war against the Indians because of the natural right to engage in fellowship and communication (de Vitoria 1967, 3.1). The Indians, however, had not prevented such fellowship and this title was invalid.

The second possible title justified conquest if the right to spread the Christian faith was being resisted (de Vitoria 1967, 3.2). The Indians, however, were amenable to hearing the gospel and had not interfered in the evangelization of the friars. This title, too, could not be used. The third possible title allows conquest if leaders of Indian converts try to bring them back to idolatrous practices. Yet how can one wage war against a fellow Christian, even if he or she is a convert? This title, also, could not be used as justification for war upon the Indians. The fourth possible title was the papal right to remove a non-Christian leader and put in his place a Christian prince (de Vitoria 1967, 3.4). This obviously was not the case in conquered America. For the same reason, one can dismiss the next possible title: the defense of innocent Indians from tyrannical leaders or laws (ibid., 3.5).

The next possible title follows closely on the last two. Justification for war upon the Indians might have been possible if the Indians governed by barbarian leaders wished to be governed by civilized Spain (ibid., 3.6). The

Encomienda, however, invalidates this title. It had been instituted without their consultation. The next possible title would allow conquest for reason of alliance and friendship (ibid., 3.7). Vitoria is referring here to Cortez' alliance with the independent Tlaxcaltecs against Moctezuma's Aztec confederacy (Corts 1986, 58-72). This, of course, did not apply in postconquest America.

All seven possible titles for just war were applied by Vitoria, and all were found wanting. Vitoria then suggested another possibility, an eighth title not based on a juridical principle but on an anthropological novelty.[24] The Amerindians, Vitoria argued, were thought incapable of managing even their own households, nor did they possess letters, arts and crafts, systematic agriculture, or manufacture.[25] Nonetheless, says Vitoria, these are not natural slaves.[26] Thus the Amerindian is not, as Las Casas argued, simply like us. They do not possess the Aristotelian marks for a civilization, yet they are not Sepúlveda's homunculi, either. They are more like children (*infantes*). To prove his point, Vitoria puts forth his famous example (Padgen 1981, 3.17.19-35):

Suppose that for some reason all the adults of those regions [America] perished and only the children (pueri) and adolescents who had some use of reason remained but still between the years of infancy (pueritiae) and puberty. It seems clear that the princes could take them under their tutelage and rule them while they were in such a state. If this is admitted, it seems certain that one cannot deny that the same could be done with the parents of these barbarians because of the mental incapacity attributed to them by those who live there which they say is much more than that of children of other nations.

Vitoria, then, argued that the Amerindian were not so much natural slaves but natural children (*pueri*) (Padgen 1986, 102).

Children, however, were seen by Aristotle as little more than animals as long as their reason remained in a state of becoming. But what could prevent these natural children from actualizing the potentiality of their reason? The answer apparently lay in a much discussed case: Lycurgus' dogs.

Tradition has it that Lycurgus reared two dogs from the same litter. One was bred for hunting and the other as a pet. When they reached adulthood, they had acquired entirely different natures (Padgen 1986, 100).[27] Such consideration led Vitoria to believe that the Amerindian's reason had kept itself only in potential due to their poor and barbaric education (de Vitoria 1967, 3.15.19). Education had a particular meaning for Vitoria. Education was more than simple schooling. Education consisted of what Aristotle called habituation (*ethismos*) which was the training of the mind (the speculative intellect) to deduce the law of nature (Padgen 1986, 99). Lycurgus' dogs and Aristotle's ethismos came together for Vitoria to produce a protomodern understanding of culture.

The Amerindian was truly different from the Iberian not because of a different humanity but of a newly identified cause of difference, a mixture of races or custom and habituation, what we today would call "culture."[28] Vitoria found a "solution" to the anthropological challenge of difference: the natural child kept inferior by the phenomenon of culture. As such, it would be proper conduct for the princes to govern them, for then it would be a "precept of charity" (de Vitoria 1967, 3.17, 38-39).

Vitoria's anthropological solution was well meant. He had been offended by the abuses of the Encomienda and had tried to protect the Amerindian from the abuses of the encomenderos by placing the Amerindian's destiny at the hands of the Crown. Moreover, he had discerned correctly that the people of America were truly different from Iberians.

These two elements proved to be a powerful persuasive force for the Crown. It now could justify its empire before the entire European world. It could also maintain control of its colonists, reap the wealth of America without qualm, and also fulfill its mission to evangelize the Amerindian. Vitoria's solution may have been a solution for the Iberians, but not for the Amerindian or the sub-Saharan African that would soon join them in America.

THE AFTERMATH OF THE VALLADOLID DEBATE

Vitoria's solution had an unforeseen effect. The global wanderings of Portugal and Spain were expanding the world beyond America. Sub-Saharan Africa, in a sense, was as much a "new" world as America. The same could be said for the Pacific.[29] Spain's "mission" had gone, unexpectedly, from putting together a nation from lands wrested from the infidel Moors to putting together an empire from an unimaginable diversity of peoples and religions. A universal anthropology created out of the theological paradigm of rationality became the basis for that empire.

As such, the *Iberian* soon became the "parent" of other natural "children," namely, the sub-Saharan African slave and the peasant Iberian Creole born in the Americas. Indeed, America itself became an immature natural child.[30] Vitoria's solution also became a solution for justifying the slavery of sub-Saharan Africans. Their slavery at one time had been rationalized as just war against an infidel nation, the Moors (Rout 1976, 11-22). The struggle against the Moors, however, was now a distant memory. Moreover, Iberia soon realized that sub-Sahara Africa was also new territory. Soon the sub-Saharan African also came to be seen under the same category as the Amerindian, a natural child.[31] A survey of attitudes toward the African in the sixteenth century supports this assertion. Thus:

Africanus in the middle of the sixteenth-century who declared that the Negroes not only led a beastly life but "were utterly destitute of reason"; and it was Peter Heylyn and Daniel Beeckman who, many years later, aided in the dissemination of the same idea. Said Heylyn in 1652, the inhabitants of Terra Nigritarum "were for the most part so rude and barbarous, that they seem to want that use of Reason, which is peculiar unto man." Said Beeckman of the Hottentots in 1714: "These filthy animals . . . hardly deserve the name of rational creatures," a sentiment which was to be revived in the Southern states just before the Civil War and which was incorporated in early American ethnology. (Hodgen 1964, 412)

This sentiment was translated into slavery. A problem loomed, however, for the interests of slavery and empire: the great Mestizaje of the Americas.

What, exactly, is the product of a natural child and that of Iberian blood? The question proved to be the most serious weapon against slavery and was attacked the most virulently.[32] Legislation after legislation in the increasingly mestizo New World was passed to prevent further Mestizaje:

If these men were born of legitimate wedlock and had no other vices or defects, they could be regarded as citizens of those provinces and could be admitted to honor and office in them, as argued by Victoria and Zapata. . . . But because they are most often born out of adultery or other illicit unions, since few Spaniards of honorable position will marry Indian or Negro women . . . they bear the taint of illegitimacy and other vices which they take in, as it were, with their milk. And these men, I find by many other decrees, are forbidden to hold any responsible public office, whether it is that of Protector of the Indians, councilman, or notary public. . . . There are other decrees that forbid them to take holy orders, unless by special dispensation. . . . But returning to the question of curacies, although for the reason given above it would be convenient to entrust them to mestizos, great care must be taken with this, for we see that the majority of them come from a vicious and depraved environment, and it is they who do the most harm to the Indians. . . . (Keen 1986, 120-21)

Even freedom or manumission did not prevent the mulatto from bearing such a social stigma.[33] St. Martín de Porres, a free mulatto, fit this category. Yet Indians, Africans, mestizos, and mulattos were not the only ones affected by Vitoria's solution.

The paradigm of rationality in the service of empire was constructing colonial Latin American society and absorbing all who were weak or marginal to peninsular Iberian society. Soon after the conquest of America, a rise in the number of "idlers, beggars, vagabonds, and criminals" occurred. These consisted of Spanish or Portuguese fortune seekers whose fortunes turned the wrong way and ended up in a life of poverty and crime (Haslip-Viera 1986, 286). This was the underclass that, as shall be seen, ended up at the kitchen door of St. Martín's kitchen.

Yet it would be misleading to leave the impression that the only consequence, tragic as it is, of non-Europeans in the New World was social prejudice. There was a more sinister dimension. The anthropology that was the foundation of this social prejudice spilled over into the religious sphere. It was more than the social question of an underclass. It was, more significantly, a theological question about New World humanity.

The theological ramifications of Vitoria's solution soon came to the surface in the furious debate among the clergy about the worthiness of Amerindians, Africans, and Mestizos to receive the sacraments. Robert Ricard (1966, 122) describes the situation with respect to the Eucharist.

> Some religious were of the opinion that they could not be admitted to the communion table, that they had been too recently converted, that they were incapable of knowing the value and grandeur of the sacrament, and that it should be denied them lest they fall into frequent sacrileges.[34]

Father Alonso de Sandoval (1627, Bk.3, Ch.12, 285) describes a similar situation with respect to the Africans.

> The negroes are indeed really capable of receiving the Faith. A great sign of this intelligence is to see how often and with what tenderness and joy they repeat the sweet name of Jesus when they are being punished, when they are ill and most especially when they are about to die, which I have often heard one of them in this predicament repeated several times in his own language: "God created me, God carries me away, what can I do?" . . . From this and many other things, two conclusions follow: one that these negroes are not brute beasts, as I have heard some say, for hereabouts they try to make out that they are incapable of being Christians, nor must they be reputed childish or defective mentally, because they are grown-up men and as such they should be given baptism, preceded by an act of will on their part and the other necessary acts, etc.

These "grown-up" men, unfortunately, were up against the new cosmic hierarchy in which they were seen as natural children.

Such is the violent and unequal encounter of cultures which created the cultural mosaic of the beatification process of St. Martín de Porres. The "little stories" refer to this dimension in one way or another. Indeed it would be difficult to undertake a reading of the "little stories" without having examined this dimension. Yet the meaning of the "little stories" cannot be found at this level. One must now turn to reading the signs, codes, and messages of the cultural mosaic created in the violent and unequal encounter of cultures.

5

Dog Stories and a Ladder

The human penchant for dogs ought to make us wonder. The *Proceso*'s penchant for dogs, on the other hand, ought to make us sit straight and take note. Story after story in the beatification process of St. Martín de Porres tells stories about dogs as well as a great variety of animals. It is well known that St. Martín loved animals. He was known as the St. Francis of the Americas (no mean feat for a Dominican). He especially loved dogs. Other than being sentimental anecdotes, what could these "little stories" about dogs and animals mean? The semiotics of culture would ask that notice be taken. Animals, especially dogs, may be important tiles or semiotic domains in the cultural mosaic of the beatification process.

"THESE KNOW ME"

The following "little stories" illustrate the point. A fellow friar, Fray Fernando de Aragones, recounts the following story.

> When he would enter the chicken house of the infirmary, the chickens would rush toward him and cuddle up next to him and would let him pick them up and pet them and delighted by his company would act as if they had been loved dearly by him. And when he entered the stables the mules and the other beasts would lovingly and docilely come to him with signs of love and affection toward him. The same occurred with dogs, cats, and other house animals who exhibited great commotion when they saw him and rushed to him giving signs of their great affection for him nudging or licking him.

This "little story" presents us with an explosion of animal activity.

Chickens madly cluck in recognition of St. Martín and fly into his arms. The mules nuzzle against him when he walks into the barn. They all seem to be saying, "Look at him, look at him." It is hard to miss what this means. The animals themselves seem to be saying, "We are signs pointing to what St. Martín is about." Support for this impression comes from the fact that the word *mulatto* derives from the word "mula" or mule. There are, in fact, several "little stories" about St. Martín and the mules. Nonetheless, there is no need at this point to go deeper into the significance of mules. It is enough to note the effect St. Martín has on animals and how this "little story" makes a point of it. An investigator looking for signs does not have to put forth much effort to see the signprints of a semiotic domain in these stories of mules and animals.

Another "little story" is told by Francisco Pérez Quintero, born in Spain and living as a master carpenter in Lima. Sr. Quintero tells this "little story" about animals.

And when this witness was sick in the infirmary, he saw that every night a large white, black, and brown cat would come through a vent that opened into the cell and walk up to said venerable brother fray Martín de Porras. When he had reached him, the cat would begin to pull on his habit with his hands as if he were giving [St. Martín] signs that it was time for some duty and said venerable brother fray Martín de Porras would leave the cell to ring the dawn bell to which he was devoted. And he did this because of said cat.

Given the previous discussion of the violent encounter of Iberian, sub-Saharan African, and Amerindian cultures, the appearance of the white, black, and brown cat is striking. Does the cat point to St. Martín's society, to the violent and unequal encounter of cultures? This "mestizo" cat, after all, wakes up the other mestizo, the mulatto Martín, and "reminds" him of his duty, a duty he loves to do. By ringing the dawn bell, St. Martín wakes up the friars from their sleep. The cat makes a point of waking up St. Martín on time so that he may ring that bell. It is responsible for waking up the Church from her sleep to begin a new day. This white, black, and brown cat signifies something to do with the bell, usually a harbinger of important news or, more significantly, the transmitter of an important message.

Cats are not the only animals that appear in the "little stories." Marcelo de Ribera, St. Martín's doctor-teacher, remembers the following incident.

And one day said servant of God became disgusted by the damage the mice had made with the clothing for the sick. He picked up a mouse and said to him "Brother, why did you and your friends damage the clothing for the sick? I won't kill you, because I want you to go and gather all your friends and go into the garden where I will bring food for all of you every day." And so it was, that from the scraps of the food from the infirmary, he brought them every day their ration and Our Lord because of the merit of [Martín's] great charity allowed it to happen that no more mice were found in the clothing room, which this witness saw for himself.

This "little story" is an example of the dynamics of a cultural mosaic. It reveals semiotic activity that is transforming meanings in response to cultural stress. Martín apparently could speak to mice. That the mice could understand St. Martín is even more surprising. Such a tale is more than a charming anecdote. This is an obvious case of a code reversal. Human beings, in most cultural mosaics, do not speak to mice, and mice do not listen to human beings. As such, more evidence presents itself that animals are important signs involving significant transformation, transformation indicated by such code reversals.

Having spoken of cats and mice, it is only natural to present the following "little story" about dogs. The following story comes from Catalina de Porras, daughter of Martín's sister, Juana.

And so great was the charity of said venerable brother Fray Martín, not only with his neighbor but also with the brute animals, that having been given an order by the Provincial of his Order to throw out from the cloister all the dogs he kept there, he was moved with compassion and pity. Thus, he took all the dogs he could find and took them to the house of the mother of this witness where he kept them tied up and those who were sick he cured . . . [One day] the mother of this witness asked him why he kept bringing so many dogs to her house. They made her angry since they soiled the house. He then told her that he was looking for a new place for them. Then he went outside and talked with the dogs telling them that when they had a necessity to go, to do it in the street outside and this witness saw that since that moment said dogs when they had a necessity to go would leave the yard and do it in the street outside and then come back without making anyone in the house angry nor soiling the house like before.

This story by Martín's niece is not only charming but telling. Martín's dogs do not seem to be wanted by anybody except by St. Martín. Even his sister did not want them. At one point, she asks, "What is it with the dogs? Why the concern?" The answer is subtle. Simply because of doing their natural thing—dogs after all, have to "go"—they were sent outside. Simply because of their being dogs, they were treated miserably. As such, a code is suggested: "being natural belongs outside."

At first glance, such a code seems reasonable. The natural does belong outside. The nature of dogs, however, compromises the meaning of such a code. Dogs, after all, are also natural inside. Dogs are domestic animals. Moreover, such a code is present alongside a code reversal, another instance of St. Martín talking to animals. Whatever dogs signify, they are pointing to concerns about the natural and the outside, on the one hand, and the human and the inside, on the other. The code reversal points to significant transformations taking place; thus the concern of Juana. These "natural" associations are apparently being transformed by St. Martín and his dogs.

Moreover, the close association of St. Martín and dogs suggests that dogs may point to St. Martín himself. This conjecture is supported by the following "little stories." Padre Fray Gerónimo Baptista de Barnuy, a fellow Dominican, testified

> that this witness saw that on many occasions the Prelates and some of the religious, in order to mortify said venerable brother fray Martín de Porras, would mean-mouth him calling him mulatto dog (*perro mulato*) and other names and he always responded with much modesty and humility and that he knew that he already was a mulatto dog.

Another fellow Dominican, Padre Fray Alonso de Arenas y Añano, recounts a similar story.

> And [he saw] that some religious of said convent who had asked him to do certain things for them, because he did not do them as fast as they liked, mean-mouthed him calling him mulatto dog (*perro mulato*) and other injurious names which he bore with the greatest humility and would say "These know me," and then gave many thanks to Our Lord.

These are but a few of many such "little stories" which, in effect, give St. Martín a name: "Mulatto dog." In one story, St. Martín responds "these know me." It is as if St. Martín is saying, "that's right, dogs signify me." These stories, then, provide enough evidence of the importance of dogs in the "little stories" of St. Martín.

ANIMAL SYMBOLS

So far an initial inventory of signifiers turns up animals, especially dogs. An initial conclusion might be that this inventory of animal signs corresponds to a major semiotic domain, the "animal domain." The conclusion, however, must be qualified because there is a complication. St. Martín's Lima was a great Mestizaje of cultures. Indigenous, African, and Iberian blood mixed to produce a marvelously varied humanity. A question can then be asked: Are animals and dogs also important signs in all the three major cultures, and, if so, what meanings do they have in common?

The answer is not, of course, the simple intersection of "animal" domain signifiers from three separate cultures. The signifiers in the *Proceso*'s animal domain will be more of a synthesis than an intersection.[1] Yet it would be helpful to take a brief look at each culture separately for signifiers found in their animal domain in order to clarify and give priority to similar signifiers in the animal domain of the *Proceso*.

The *Encyclopedia of Religion* tells that animals are core symbols in most cultures. Thus

> Wherever they appear, animal symbols are used to convey the deepest and most abstruse dimensions of human existence. They are symbols of core values and categories, representations of the most fundamental ideas and images of a culture. As core symbols, they are multivalent, complex, antinomic, used simultaneously to capture and display many different images and meanings at many different levels. As core symbols, they also serve to link other domains of symbolic discourse, creating juxtapositions and contrasts of images from which people derive meaning and from which they generate narrative forms . . . Animal symbols are often used to express the fundamental ideas of selfness and otherness that lie at the basis of moral and religious thought. In being both similar to humans in some ways and dissimilar in others, animals provide the basis for many other dialectic aspects of human thought and may represent categories of sacred and profane, wild and civilized, natural and cultural, immoral and moral, inchoate and formed, material and essential, mundane and divine. Animal symbols represent the antinomies of living, the existence of the sacred in the profane, the wild in the civilized, the immoral in the moral. Thus, people are able to use animal symbols to create analogies that can be extended to the relationships of humans to the divine. (Walens 1986, 291)

Among the animal symbols in the "little stories" of St. Martín, the dog stands out. Dogs, as general symbols, occupy an ambivalent position.

> As the companion of hunters and herders, the dog became a symbol of fidelity and vigilance. As a predator and scavenger, however, it has been seen as greedy, dangerous, and impure . . . The dog becomes in some societies a culture hero: in Maya manuscripts it brings maize to mankind . . . and in extensive areas of Africa, it imparts knowledge of edible plants . . . Also widespread is the belief in the dog as ancestor of man . . . From the coasts of the southwestern Pacific to as far as North America there are myths in which the ancestress of a tribe married a dog. (Lurker 1986)

From this general survey, certain points about the semiosphere of the cultural mosaic connected with St. Martín de Porres can be made. Animals, especially dogs, could well be the core symbol or root metaphor that gives rise to the semiosphere. Dogs, above all, signify fundamental anthropologies in all the cultures of the mosaic.

One can be more specific in terms of the specific cultures. Fr. Bernabé Cobo, the early priest-anthropologist, mentions that Andeans made a distinction between domestic and wild animals. Moreover, domestic animals had to do with the "health and affairs of men" (1990, 113). The "little stories" of St. Martín, in fact, refer solely to domesticated animals. Mules, bulls, chickens, dogs, cats, and mice are the animals that inhabit the semiosphere of the "little stories" of St. Martín. As such, they may refer to a possible meaning. The "little stories" are being used to say something about the health of human affairs.

The Andeans also had ambivalent attitudes about dogs. According to Garcilaso de la Vega, a mestizo chronicler of that era, dogs were worshiped for their "faithfulness and nobility" (1966, 31). The howling of a dog, however, was seen as an omen of death or harm. Thus, the Andeans made sacrifices to the dog to harm their enemies and not them (Cobo 1979, 113). There also exists accounts of Amerindians actually communicating with ferocious dogs to calm them down or deflect their anger. Gerbi (1985, 353) recounts this tale from Oviedo's *Historia Natural*:

> Equally sympathetic is the tale of the old Indian woman who Diego de Salazar decided to feed to his savage dogs. The beldam was given a letter to take to the governor, a league away, and as she set off with the message, "going very happily along, because she thought that for delivering the letter they were setting her free," he unleashed his mastiff after her. When the old lady saw that she was being followed she sat down on the ground and began to talk to the hound in her own language, "Good master dog, I am taking this letter to the governor"; and she showed it the letter or paper clutched in her hand and said to it, "Don't harm me, Mr. dog." And the dog in fact stopped, then approached her "and cocked a leg and piddled on her," as dogs do at the corners of houses, but otherwise left her unharmed. And the terrified old woman...was spared her life by the Spaniards.

Africa also has its animal symbols. Fear of revenge from a killed or wounded animal governs the attitude toward animals in the hunting societies of Africa. Hunters try to mediate this fear by singing their thanks to the killed animal (Zerries 1986, 24). Most of the African slaves came to America from Western Africa, and many belonged to the Yoruba tribe. Yoruba beliefs, then, can be indicative of African cultural symbols in the New World.

The Yoruba, for example, held the dog in special esteem because of the god Ogun. Ambivalence characterized Ogun. He destroyed and protected at the same time. The celebration of an annual Ogun festival assured good game for hunting through animal sacrifice. This ritual sacrifice of animals says much about Yoruban animal symbolism.

> In general, ritual sacrifice accomplishes a two-way transaction between two otherwise separate and partially opposed realms: the world of man and the world of gods. In this transaction, the animal victim is the mediating symbol because it partakes of both worlds. It lives in the human world, but its life belongs to the spiritual world. Furthermore it combines certain symbolic features which link the human with the divine so that the divine is subject to human control. In this way, the ritual manipulation of the sacrificial victim helps men mediate their relation to the gods. (Ray 1976, 78-9)

As such, the dog had special meaning for the Yoruba people.

> Above all, it is the dog which is especially noted as Ogun's sacrifice. The dog appears to be uniquely appropriate because it combines in itself both the wildness and ferocity of its natural state and the friendliness and protectiveness of its domestic state. In this respect, the dog symbolically corresponds to Ogun's dualistic, destructive/protective nature and is therefore a most suitable medium for establishing and controlling intimate contact with him. *In a wider sense, as elements of nature transformed by human contact into elements of culture, the offerings are appropriate mediating symbols between nature and culture, divinity and humanity* [emphasis mine]. (Ray 1976, 80-1)

The Ibero-European semiosphere had its share of animal symbolism as well. In general, animals often symbolized vices or virtues often characterized in the bestiaries of the Middle Ages. Animals often signified saints (Cret 1907). The East influenced Ibero-European tradition through 700 years of contact with Islam. Thus, one needs to look at the way the dog was viewed in the East to appreciate its place in the Ibero-European tradition.

> The dog in the East does not enjoy the companionship and friendship of man as in the western countries. Its instinct has been cultivated only in so far as the protecting of the flocks and camps against wild animals is concerned. In the towns and villages it roams in the streets and places, of which it is the ordinary scavenger; packs of dogs in a half-wild state are met with in the cities and are not infrequently dangerous for men. For this reason the dog has always been, and is still looked upon with loathing and aversion, as filthy and unclean . . . the Mohammedans, to the present day, term Christian "dogs." (Souvay 1907, 521)

When one realizes that Iberians often characterized any black African as a Moor (Muslim), the significance of dogs in the "little stories" of the mulatto St. Martín takes on added dimensions. Dogs were also used to wage war or to signify relentlessness in pursuit. The Dominicans, for example, in relentless pursuit of true doctrine, were known as the "hounds of God." The Spanish used ferocious mastiffs in war against the Amerindian (León-Portilla 1963).

A general survey of the "animal" domain points to the centrality of dogs in all three semiospheres as signifiers of social and anthropological statements. The use of dogs in the "little stories" of the *Proceso* is an important signifier that calls for special attention. Moreover, if anything new is being said about human being in the "little stories" of the *Proceso,* it will be said through the signs belonging to the animal domain.

Two conclusions can be made. First, dogs are signifiers common to all three semiospheres. Thus, all members of Lima's society participate in the signification going on in the "little stories" of the *Proceso.* Second, dogs are primal signifiers of human being. As such, they are capable of constructing new meanings of the human. Thus, the use of dogs in the "little stories" of the *Proceso* points to places of transformation where new meanings about human being are being formed.

HEALING DOGS AS IF THEY WERE PEOPLE

A search for metaphors in the "little stories" of the *Proceso* is another step in identifying important semiotic domains.[2] Such a study of the "little stories" reveals metaphors that are repeated over and over again. The Procurator General of St. Martín's Order, Fray Antonio de Estrada, once again offers a "little story." "He also gave many alms to a great number of poor and sick, the same with Spaniards as with Indians and Blacks, and even, with the brute animals, these he cured with the same care as if they were rational men."

Fray Francisco de Arce repeats a similar tale. "And his great charity and burning zeal was not only used with his neighbors and rational brothers but also with the irrational ones, curing them when he saw them sick and giving them food and sustenance."

Fray Fernando Aragones testified:

And so all the friars, Indians and blacks, small and big, all took him as father, for relief and comfort through his works [of healing]; and this was not a miracle, for they were capable of reason; what seems out of all course and all that is natural is to see the animals who in not having any [reason], nor being capable of it, to recognize in said servant of God this charity.

These "little stories" are, perhaps, the most numerous in the *Proceso*—thus their importance as indicators of semiotic domains. The recurrent metaphor is of healing, but it compares or links two other metaphors—"irrational (brute) animals" and "rational men." It could be stated as healing-irrational-animals-as-if-they-were-rational-men. The metaphor of healing, in effect, maps the animal domain into the man or human domain. Such mapping means that the man domain is undergoing considerable transformation. This provides another clue to the structure of the cultural mosaic. Transformation of meaning corresponds to the shifting of boundaries, so the mapping above suggests the presence of a semiotic boundary. But where?

First, consider that two semiotic domains have been mentioned: man and animal. As such, they may be envisioned as major tiles in our cultural mosaic. Second, a boundary is indicated by the mapping. The mapping of irrational animals to rational men suggests the binary opposition, "irrational"/"rational." This semiotic boundary may be envisioned as the grout between the two major tiles discovered above. Put together, the mosaic structure of the "little stories" of St. Martín can be envisioned as an animal tile adjacent to a man tile separated by the boundary "irrational"/"rational."

Apparently, the binary opposition "rational"/"irrational" separates the animal domain from the man domain. It is not a structure, however, that is supposed to remain fixed. The healing metaphor serves to map each domain across this boundary and, in doing so, creates a new domain. The healing metaphor, in other words, is combining these two important tiles of our mosaic to form a new tile. What this new tile may be can be deduced from an examination of the healing domain.

Healing is a metaphor with profound meanings. The anthropology of healing provides some general guidelines toward determining those meanings: "rituals of healing redress the fragmented social, personal, temporal, physical, and metaphysical tissues constituting the whole of the universe" (Sullivan 1986, 233).

This comes about by a connection made between physiologies and the universe. Thus:

Cosmologies and physiologies are cultural constructs that offer systematic appraisals of the order in which disease insinuates itself to inspire disorder . . . The body serves as a microcosm where the powers of disease can be located, contested, pacified, eliminated, or accommodated . . . The cultural rendering of the dynamics of the body fan outward to relate patients and doctors to the organized processes of the world. (Calame-Griaule 1986, 368)

Thus, healing relates the human being to cosmic order. People, when sick, often feel out of sorts or sense that something is not in order with their body. Moreover, "the powers of healing are often exemplary beings who serve as models for medical practice." Among these powers of healing one can include "saints renowned for cure" (Calame-Griaule 1986, 367). Related to the metaphor of healing is an African understanding of illness. Illness, in many African cultures, has moral and religious dimensions (Ray 1976, 80-1). Illness is more than a disorder of the body. It is a disorder of society as well. In the African semiosphere, signs of illness are also signs of social disorder. The metaphor of healing has profound meanings related to the perceived social and natural order of things.

THE DEMON AND THE LADDER

Such meanings as those found in the healing domain are also found in the Ibero-European man domain. The Ibero-European man domain, for example, also says something about cosmic order. Cosmic order for Ibero-Europeans begins with the distinguishing place of the human being. Far superior to the animals but a little lower than the angels, the human being was the ordering principle of the cosmos. This ordering principle was known as the hierarchy of being.[3]

The hierarchy of being was a ubiquitous ordering principle of Ibero-European society during the sixteenth and seventeenth centuries. Its roots can be traced to Pseudo-Dionysius (Leclercq 1987, 25-32), but its formative stages took place in the twelfth century (Chenu 1968). The hierarchy of being envisioned a cosmic "ladder" of being which progressed from animals to humans to angels. Through this principle, Thomas Aquinas entertained the nature of the cosmic order in the *Summa* (1964, 1a, q.50): "the distinction of corporeal and spiritual creatures: firstly, the purely spiritual creature which in Holy Scripture is called angel; secondly, the creature wholly corporeal; thirdly, the composite creature, corporeal and spiritual, which is man."

The animals followed a natural progression to the spiritual with man at the boundary between the corporal and the spiritual. This boundary was the faculty of reason. Below that boundary dwelt irrational beings; above it rational beings. At the boundary stood man. Thus the theologian-philosopher Boethius defined man as "an individual substance of a rational nature."[4] This suggests a connection between the binary opposition "rational"/"irrational" of the "little stories" and the Ibero-European "Big Story" of human being distinguished by the boundary between irrational and rational beings.

As such, the metaphorical mapping, healing-irrational-animals-as-if-they-were-rational-men, may be construed as constructing a new "Big Story" of human being, a "Big Story" different from the Ibero-European. Such construction takes place on two fronts. First, "little stories" of healing cross the boundary separating the animal domain from the man domain. The net effect is the remapping of elements from an old (Old World) anthropology into a new (New World) anthropology. Second, the binary opposition "rational"/"irrational" that defines and separates the man domain from the animal domain in the Ibero-European definition of human being is challenged or reinterpreted.

Semiotically, this involves the shifting of boundaries. This can be done by mapping one boundary with another. Just as two domains may be mapped by another, two semiotic boundaries may be mapped by a third. Such an operation can take place through a sequence of binary parallels that involves the reversal of the middle term. Thus the binary oppositions "mighty"/"lowly" and "first"/"last" may be mapped by means of a third binary opposition, say, "up"/"down." The mighty are associated with high places. They are first to be seated in places of high honor. The lowly, on the other hand, are associated with low places. The lowly, in fact, must bow down before the mighty. This state of affairs can be changed by introducing codes which reverse the meaning of up and down.

In the Magnificat, for example, the lowly are lifted up and the mighty brought down. Such a code reversal has an effect on the binary opposition "first"/ "last." The reversal of "up"/"down" means that a new parallelism has been established: "up"/"down" now parallels "lowly"/"mighty." This new parallelism communicates a startling transformation: "lowly"/"mighty" parallels "up"/"down," which now parallels "first"/"last" or, in the words of the gospels, "the first shall be last, and the last shall be first." Such operations are common in the semiotics of culture, and the alert investigator will keep an eye open for such transformations in the "little stories."

Another step in Schreiter's semiotics of culture identifies the codes operative in the cultural mosaic. Some have been mentioned. The *Proceso* contains various codes and messages which, at times, overlap. The various codes and messages often build on other codes and messages, and in their totality tell a story. The process of semiosis cannot be neatly dissected and then put back together again. Simple codes and messages lay the foundation for narrative, and these narratives lay the foundations for larger narratives and, in turn, more complex codes and messages. The cascading effect is what Geertz called a "thick" interpretation (as opposed to a scientific "thin" description) full of imagery and connections (1973, 5-7). The prize, however, for our semiotic analysis is the principal code of the "little stories" of St. Martín. What, in the end, is the "grammar" of the "little stories"? The answer may lie in an important sixteenth-century metaphor for the hierarchy of being: the ladder.[5]

If healing is a principal metaphor, then the infirmary of St. Martín's convento should be an important place. This suspicion is confirmed by the following story told by Captain Juan de Cordoba Guarnido:

And so declares as public and notarized comment that it was told there was a ladder in the convent which descended from a high alcove into the infirmary which was ordinarily closed for use for various reasons, and when, occasionally, they did open the passage it was only by a stroke of good luck that someone did not fall or was hurt in doing so. On one occasion going up the said ladder the venerable brother Fray Martín de Porras, who was going to the aid of a sick religious who was in need at the late hours of the night with a candle brazier in one hand and also some clothing, found himself with the devil and asked him what he was doing there to which the demon responded that through this passageway he made his earnings from those who would cross it. And having told [the devil] to go back to his deep, cursed caverns, [the devil] didn't want to do it and so [St. Martín] took off his belt and hit him with it saying many words and [the devil] left. With the coals in the brazier, [St. Martín] made two crosses which this witness saw on the wall . . . And that the said venerable brother, after the aforementioned, ordered a wooden cross about a "vara y media" [about five feet, or the height of a man] in height and put it in the same place as the ones he had made with the coal which this witness also saw. And from then on, there was passage through said ladder without anyone getting hurt unlike as before.

Thus the infirmary is a site where struggle with demons occur, and the struggle takes place on a ladder that descends from a high place. Indeed, it was on his way to help a sick brother that St. Martín encountered the demon on the ladder. The code begins to emerge. St. Martín's healing is also a message about the demon who lives on the ladder.

This demon makes people fall from the ladder, wounding them in the process of making his *ganancias* (earnings). The ladder, then, is a place in St. Martín's world where a demon makes a living out of wounding and hurting people. The ladder, however, is also a metaphor for the hierarchy of being. This is suggested by the height of the cross St. Martín places on the wall—five feet, the height of a human being. This sugggests the principal code of the "little stories": the hierarchy of being is a ladder where a demon dwells, hurting people who try to climb it. The crucial height of the ladder is at five feet, the place of the human. St. Martín's actions, as recounted in the "little stories," are to be understood in terms of this code.

The code, then, consists of a demon and a ladder. As such, it is not a full condemnation of the hierarchy of being but of some element in it. Something in the hierarchy of being is hurting or wounding people. St. Martín's struggle is not so much against the hierarchy of being as with some demonic element within it. This demonic element has to do with the height of humanity on the ladder. Something is wrong in the cosmic place of human being in the order of things. More needs to be said. The cultural mosaic of the *Proceso* continues to be uncovered as more "little stories" are told.

6

The Ill and the Wounded

The "little stories" of St. Martín de Porres have revealed part of their mosaic structure—a ladder. On that ladder stands a demon who is hurting the people of Lima. A question, however, remains: Who or what is the demon? A thorough look at the whole *Proceso* uncovers a significant number of stories possessing strikingly similar structure and themes. A recurring pattern consists of a subtle yet striking contrast between the healing of the friars and well-to-do of Lima's society and the poor, the Indios, the Negros, and those of mixed race, the mestizo and mulatto.

THE ILL

The illnesses suffered by the friars and the well-to-do of Lima who came to St. Martín are various and illuminating. Fray Fernando Aragones tells this "little story" of a friar ill with a fever.

> And being sick in a cell with two religious, one of them having been very sick and the other a novice called fray Francisco Martínez. The novice made fun of some gibberish said while the other was suffering from a fever, and said servant of God, fray Martín de Porras, having heard it told [the novice]: "Brother, try to commend yourself to God for this religious has already escaped danger and I don't know if the brother will also." And when the fourteenth day of the illness of said fray Francisco Martínez came, he died.

Fevers are dangerous. They can kill. Moreover, fever, at its climax, can cause one to utter irrational gibberish. This is fever's most dangerous point. One friar did not seem to recognize the seriousness of the symptom but laughed naïvely at the other's perilous condition. St. Martín warned him, but the danger was not recognized. The friar died when he reached the same point. This "little story" suggests a code. St. Martín was the knowledgeable doctor familiar with fevers (*calenturas*) that affected, above all, the friars and well-to-do. The most mortal moment is the moment of madness, of gibberish, when a rational being is turned into an irrational one.

The fevers of the monks made them irrational. Fevers, however, are not so much a disease but the symptom of a disease. The symptom is detected at the forehead through a hotness to the touch. As such, fevers are a symptom of a sick society that is hurting people. This symptom also involves a "hotness," a demon, in the area of the body associated with the seat of reason, the forehead, the five-foot level of the hierarchy of being. The fevers point to the demon on the ladder. This demon in the ladder of being makes Ibero-Europeans ill and wounds the poor or mixed race of the New World. This demon is the "irrational"/"rational" distinction in the hierarchy of being that determines whether one is human or not. If, as a human, one is deemed irrational, death inevitably follows.

The fevers of the monks are signs which also have a history. They point to a moment in time: the violent and unequal encounter of cultures that was characterized by great epidemics. A major symptom of these epidemic diseases was fever. These epidemics led to the demographic collapse of the Amerindian and the importation of sub-Saharan African slaves. Many slaves were brought to the New World already sick with African diseases such as yellow fever. These diseases went on to infect the slaver as well. Fevers are an example of a historical sign, that is, a historical element which is also a sign. The fevers of the monks and the well-to-do of Lima are connected with these historical events. The cultural mosaic of Lima was constructed, in part, through the sociohistorical currents that led to the catastrophic deaths of millions of Amerindians and the enforced slavery of human beings across the Atlantic.

Many of the fevers of the friars were due to some inflammation or illness of the leg. Fray Fernando del Aguila recounts such a story.

And this witness heard fray Gerónimo Baptista, a priest in the [Dominican] Order, tell that while being sick in bed with dangerous ulcers he had on one leg which a surgeon was taking care of with great care, [the ulcers on the leg] had reached such an extreme that the surgeon wanted to saw the whole leg off to prevent the cancer from threatening [his life]. When the surgeon began the process of sawing off his leg, the said venerable brother fray Martín de Porras came into the cell and asked the surgeon why he was cutting off the leg [and asked him] to stop and he would heal it, which the said servant of God did and in a few days, he was healthy and well of said leg.

Captain Juan de Figueroa tells an even more interesting story.

Once P. fray Pedro de Montesdoca, religious of this Order of our father St. Dominic, was sick in bed with an illness that came upon his leg, when said brother fray Martín de Porras came in to take care of him but because of some childishness (niñeria) which took place in the cell, said fray Pedro Montesdoca got mad at him and became disrespectful, saying he was a mulato dog and other bad things, after which said brother fray Martín left the cell laughing. On the following day, [St. Martín] with much peace and joy entered said cell with a salad of capers saying to said Padre fray Pedro de Montesdoca: "Well, father, are you still mad? Eat this little salad of capers which I bring you." And said Padre fray Pedro [was amazed] for he had wanted such a salad all day being so sick from this illness, suffering from hunger, and also the pain of knowing his leg was to be amputated the following day. So it seemed strange to him that [St. Martín] had brought him exactly what he was desiring and thinking this an act of God, he asked pardon from said brother fray Martín for the anger and the words which he had spoken and gave him thanks for the gift. [Thus] with great fervor, he asked him to take pity on him and to be aware that they were going to cut off one of his legs. At which said brother fray Martín came and saw [the leg] and put his hands on it and so [the friar] was healed and freed from danger.

There are numerous "little stories" about sick legs. There appears to have been an epidemic of leg illness in Lima. Considering the need of a good pair of legs to climb a ladder, these "little stories" about legs may tell something important about our root metaphor, the ladder, or hierarchy of being.

Martín came "in," a pattern typical of the accounts of the ill. He came into the "inside" of the cell to heal the sick which, in both cases, were ill of a gangrenous leg. We are not given much clue in the first account about the meaning of the gangrenous leg. The second account is more detailed. The gangrenous leg is connected to the good friar's impatience and irritability with St. Martín, an irritability which led the good friar to call St. Martín a mulatto dog, a story that is familiar.

The friar's irritability may be understood as an important signifier if contemporary beliefs about disease are examined. In John Archer's *Compendious Herbal* (1673, 44), a revealing statement of seventeenth-century belief about disease is articulated.

The next thing conducible to Health, having now sufficiently spoken of wholsome Air, Meat, and Drink &c. Is Passions of the Mind, and exercise of Body, the perturbations of the Mind do much hurt to the Body, as no Physician will deny, an *Enthumy* or well settled Mind, and such as is at quiet, doth very much tend to the preservation of Health, for although every man that is diseased in Body, is troubled also in Mind by the peccant humours which makes Men angry and peevish, that it makes true the saying, there can hardly be found *Mens Sana*, but in *corpore Sano*, yet there are some Men in perfect Health that wilfully take upon them such a habit or custome of Anger, that not only disturbs their own House and Relations, but thereby bring into their own Bodies Sickness and Death.

Archer's description is telling. A popular belief of the seventeenth century (and ours!) asserts that sick people are often irritable. More striking is the belief that the converse is true as well. Angry people often become sick. "Little stories" about anger are also stories about sickness. Yet more can be said.

Angry people often become irrational. You can't reason with them. Moreover, when angry people become irrational, they become extremely dangerous. Like fever, anger is also a dangerous condition. Its most dangerous point is reached when rational people turn irrational. When this happens, other people may get hurt and even die. The illness associated with the friar's leg is connected with the processes of the mind. Something is being said about the binary "irrational"/"rational" with the "little stories" about the illnesses of the leg. Deeper connections, however, are being made. A review of the context of how early medieval and Renaissance medicine understood the relationship between disease and the mind helps uncover these connections.

Early medieval and Renaissance medicine was based on what is known as the complexion theory of disease. The term *complexio* (for the Greek *crasis*) stood for "temperament." The complexion or temperament of an individual was uniquely his or her own. This temperament also varied according to environmental and geographical conditions. People who lived in cold climates had colder and moister complexions than those who lived in warmer climates. Gender also had its unique complexion. Women were cold and moist, while men were hot and dry.

Such understanding may seem inconsequential until it is realized that early medieval and Renaissance medicine also endowed the different organs of the body with their own unique complexions. The heart, for example, was hot, and the brain was cold. It doesn't take much imagination to associate a person's complexion with the characteristic complexions of the organs. A person who had a hot complexion was impulsive but had heart. A person who had a cold complexion was brainy but detached.

Other associations, however, can be made with complexion theory. An entire people may be associated with a complexion. People born in the warm climates of Peru or sub-Saharan Africa, for example, tend to be of the heart, while the people of colder Europe tend to be people of the brain. The ideal complexion, of course, was not to be too warm or too cold but just right. Thus, the various complexions that impinged on an individual through his or her own individuality, gender, and environment produced a predominant complexion that, ideally, would be well-balanced. When that balance was off, sickness occurred (Siraisi 1900, 103-3).

Two interesting details of complexion theory are pertinent to the "little stories." One was the belief that of all the species the human was the most balanced in complexion. When the friars refer to St. Martín as a dog, something is also being said about hot versus cold and impulsive versus brainy. The other detail is that the hand was considered to be the most temperate point in the body. These two details help further the connections of the "little stories" about the leg.

The interplay between anger and temperance, between an angry friar and a cool and temperate St. Martín, suggests that a constrast is being made. If anger can be associated with irrationality and collectedness with rationality, then the contrast between the complexion of the friar and that of St. Martín reveals the presence of the binary "irrrational"/"rational." This time, however, the binary is reversed in the hierarchy of being informing the social order of Lima. A mulatto represented the rational and an Ibero-European friar the irrational. More revealing, St. Martín healed the angry friar's leg by placing his hand, the most temperate part of the body, over the sick leg. The leg had become unbalanced, and St. Martín transfered his own balance or temperance to the affected part.

Through these striking contrasts, St. Martín broke the code of the hierarchy of being. What was rational now becomes irrational, and vice versa. Thus, the boundary represented by the binary "irrational"/"rational" has been crossed. By breaking the code, St. Martín reversed the Ibero-European criteria by which humanity was defined. As such, subtle semiotic shifts occurred which eventually ended up in a new criterion for humanity, a criterion emerged from the New World.

Another revealing "little story" concerns the illness of hidropesía (gout). Captain Juan de Guarnido was a witness to the events of this marvelous story.

And Fray Diego de Medrano became so sick with hidropesía that they took him to the infirmary of the convent to be healed. And in the passing of a few days, no betterment of the condition being noticed, instead [it was] getting worse, the doctors lost hope . . . and [he] was watched day and night by myself and another religious . . . when one night, having locked the door of his cell with key and crossbar, both fell asleep, and being asleep, around three in the morning, more or less, this witness felt the heat of a candle on his face, and then this witness heard [St. Martín] scolding them for being so lax in their care of said ill one. And starting a light, this witness saw St. Martín with a candle brazier in one arm along with a shirt and some sheets for said ill one who they found on the floor cold and almost dead without being able to speak. [St. Martín] had come to take care of that need without having been called. Going to look at where [St. Martín] had come in, [the witness] found the door locked the same way as when he had fallen asleep and was filled with great admiration. And the said ill one, after a few days got healed and well of the said sickness and got up from the bed giving thanks to God our Lord for having given him health.

The account reminds us of another story already heard: the demon on the ladder. There St. Martín also carried a candle brazier and some clothing on his way to heal someone. As such, a connection between St. Martín's healing of Fray Diego's hidropesía and St. Martín's struggle with the demon is being made.

Hidropesía, moreover, smells foul. St. Martín's biographer, Fray Bernardo de Medina, describes the disease and its typical cure (1964, 52-53):

There was a religious, Fray Andrés de Ulloa who suffered from a mortal hidropesía, an illness so importune, that the more you treat the symptoms the worse it gets. It is usually cured by artificially taking the water out of the patient which being in his veins corrupts even the breath of the hidropetic with its foul smell. They took a whole glass of water out of this patient but it had such a foul smell that it became intolerable not only to those present but those in neighboring cells.

Hidropesía's foul smell is a sign. Its referent may be found with the aid of an ancient tradition concerning smell.

An ancient tradition concerns the "spiritual" senses, a tradition popular in the Middle Ages. The spiritual senses are analogous to the more familiar bodily senses. St. Bernard made the analogy in a sermon that "in the same way that the body receives its senses through the soul, so does our soul receive a set of five senses, the 'spiritual' senses, from the soul of our soul, God." These five spiritual senses are "nothing more than various ways to love . . . It is the love which addresses itself to God" (Rahner 1933, 264).

The five spiritual senses were an analogy to the five corporal senses in order to translate a simple experience: no one has ever seen God, yet God remains, in a certain manner, accessible (Canvet 1936, 600). This experience, however, depends on a concept of human being. The accessibility of God to the soul is explained in the theology of the human being by the notion of the imago Dei, the image of God (Origen 1969, VI, Sc150, p.88). Thus the five spiritual senses also depend on this imago Dei. The imago Dei, however, also distinguishes us from the animals which, in the language of the hierarchy of being, concerns the distinction between the irrational and the rational.

The spiritual sense of smell, in particular, was associated with the hierarchy of being. Pseudo-Dionysius (1987, 228-9), for example, speaks of the role of smell or "fragance" in the hierarchy of being.

> In a manner appropriate to the divinity he turns to those minds which have achieved the closest conformity to God and he bestows on them an outpouring of divine fragrances to delight the intelligence, to cause a longing for God's gifts, and to feed on conceptual food. Each intellectual power is granted these fragrant outpourings in proportion to whatever part it has in the divine. Obviously those beings which are above us and which are our superiors in divinity receive, so to speak, a greater flood of fragrant odors since they are closer to the source. Such outpouring is more apparent and more readily received by these beings whose intellectual powers are fully attentive so that this flood spreads over them and generously, mightily, superabundantly enters into them. But with regard to lower and less receptive intelligent beings it conceals the pure sight and share of itself and grants to those attuned to it perfumes in accordance with the harmonious measure appropriate to the divinity.

Pseudo-Dyonisius' theory of human being spills over into popular religion through the the the odor of sanctity, a common phenomenon in the lore of popular religiosity.[1] Such a phenomenon is reported in the "little stories" of St. Martín. Doña Ursula de Medina, daughter of St. Martín's mentor, barber-surgeon Dr. Marcelo de Ribera, testifies that

> at age twelve, more or less, she found herself at the burial of said venerable fray brother Martín de Porres, and she was in the company of other women. And when she entered the cemetery of the *Convento*, she sensed a powerful smell, which did not appear to be anything found in this world, and this witness, entering the church, looked everywhere to see if she could find what was causing the smell but saw nothing. It then struck her that the smell was coming from the body of said servant of God.

Similarly, Fray Francisco de Oviedo testified that in the exhuming of St. Martín's bones

> he had to handle [St. Martín's] bones with his hands. From then on, his hands smelled like dried roses but stronger, and that after having washed his hands, this witness went to other friars who all smelled his hands and also sensed a similar fragrance [of roses].

There is no doubt that St. Martín had died in the odor of sanctity. More important, the odor was a sign referring to the hierarchy of being.

Fray Juan Ochoa de Verástegui reports a more intriguing story:

> This witness after having seen the said servant of God involved in such duty [the cleaning of toilets] thought that he would emit some bad smell but I always saw him as if he had never done such duty. [He always had] with [him] a delightful smell on his person and never with a bad smell. Also although he wore a hair shirt that stripped his skin and made him sweat profusely, this witness on embracing him always found a delightful smell on his person, by which reason makes me consider that as one who living among sinners does not sin, the same with [St. Martín] working among bad smells does not smell.

St. Martín works among bad smells, but he himself is not affected. Indeed, St. Martín "does not smell." During his lifetime, St. Martín had worked among bad smells, but now, in death, his work finished, he smelled of roses. Thus a fragrant smell signifies that St. Martín is a servant of God, as well as providing a clue as to the meaning of his life's work. What precisely that meaning is has yet to be established. If St. Martín worked among bad smells, then the meaning of St. Martín's work might be found in the meaning of bad smells.

A bad smell points to something else, something far away from God. ⅃ Moreover, hidropesía and bad smells have ancient connections. Hidropesía (gout) was known as a disease of the gluttonous, a disease of the rich (Sheldon 1988, 330). In a popular seventeenth-century treatise, gout was also called a "monster, that great enemy of mankind." More importantly, it was common belief that "fever was the mother of the gout" (Busschof 1676). Fever, as mentioned above, was a sign of the binary "irrational"/"rational." There seems to be a similar connection with gout.

The evidence is clear. Smell in the "little stories" is a sign. If a fragrant smell signifies that St. Martín is the one known for healing, then a foul smell signifies his antithesis, the demon on the ladder who makes people sick. No doubt the cell where Fray Diego lay sick was closed because the sick man's friends wanted to shut out the smell of the hidropesía from the rest of the friars. The door, however, was transparent to St. Martín. It could not hide the smell of hidropesía from him. The illnesses affecting the friars and the well-to-do are of great semiotic significance. The illnesses are associated with a grievous struggle with the devil, a struggle with a great sin that smells to high heaven, a sin that was making these people sick.

The "little story" of Fray Diego above also concerns a door. St. Martín walked through the door to reach Fray Diego. Walking through doors involves a code reversal. People do not walk through doors. Indeed, St. Martín and doors are intimately connected; he often walks through doors or walls in the "little stories." Joseph Pizarro tells such a story.

This witness while working in said convent went to the cell of said venerable brother fray Martín de Porras between eight and nine o'clock in the morning as was his custom to ask for something to eat. When he reached the cell, he saw [St. Martín] leave with some medications apparently to heal someone sick. Not wanting to detain him, this witness let him go and remained in the outside of his cell since [St. Martín] had left the door open. And having waited awhile without being distracted by anything else, he saw said venerable brother fray Martín de Porras come out from his cell from the inside and call him by name. Having seen this, the witness was terrified and marveled how said venerable brother fray Martín de Porras could have entered his cell without this witness having seen him enter through the door of the cell, since he had been standing in front of it. St. Martín, in any case, gave him something to eat and the witness left.

A similar story is told by Fray Antonio Gutiérrez.

Fray Juan Ramírez told this witness that while a novice he became ill with a serious sickness and lay in the Novitiate. In the middle of the night he became hungry and wanted to eat something when said venerable brother came in even though the doors, which were two, were locked and the Master of Novices kept the keys. And he had been astounded since it had been in the middle of the night and the Novitiate was locked and he had not told anyone about his hunger.

St. Martín, as mentioned in a previous chapter, was the Convento's doorkeeper. His function was to attend to the door that kept the outside world from the inside of the Convento. Many of the "little stories" tell how upset the friars were because St. Martín kept opening this door. St. Martín's office of doorkeeper takes on significance with the stories above. All these stories have something in common, revealing a semiotic structure. St. Martín walked in from the outside. St. Martín, however, did not mix in and out by this action so much as he walked freely through either space, even when such spaces were guarded by closed and locked doors. The message is not about dissolving differences but about the ability to traverse them. A foul smell, on the other hand, points to the demon on the ladder, about a certain greed and gluttony which somehow have taken residence in the hierarchy of being. The doors enclosing the smells were traversed by St. Martín as if they were not there. Indeed, it was St. Martín's ability to cross through them that allowed healing to take place. Moreover, doors are meant to hide the smell so it won't offend, but no smell could hide from St. Martín. The ugly secrets of the Ibero-European social order could not be hidden from St. Martín.

The ill, through the use of signs such as smell and doors, expose the demon on the ladder: the binary "irrational"/ "rational." The "little stories" of the *Proceso* keep demonstrating how St. Martín transformed those signs by continually breaking the code that gives meaning to them. Moreover, this analysis of the ill demonstrates that the notion of inside is associated with a foul smell and enclosement with a door. The ill are found inside, behind closed doors, in a state of irrationality, emitting a foul smell. As such, the ill, who for the most part represent the better-to-do of Lima—some of the most rational and civilized members in the New World—become, in the sick room, the opposite of what they represent. They now become the irrational ones, the less-civilized members of Limean society. They were healed only because St. Martín could transverse doors, was not put off by the smell, and was not displeased with their irrationality. As such, St. Martín reversed the code. What was thought rational is now irrational and vice versa.

This reversal signals that an important semiotic shift is taking place in the "little stories." A hint of how that shift is to take place has been given in another semiotic structure revealed in the stories about walking through doors and walls. This semiotic structure is the binary opposition "inside"/ "outside" which indicates the presence of a semiotic boundary. More importantly, having found another binary opposition, the possibility is opened up for a middle term by which a transformation of semiotic boundaries can take place. This possibility can be explored in the stories of the wounded.

THE WOUNDED

The medieval practice of taking the "discipline"[2] or wearing a hair shirt probably offends our modern sensibilities, yet in the time of St. Martín, it was the sign of great sanctity. In the *Proceso,* however, the disciplines and hair shirt take on new significance through the semiosis of the beatification process. Account after account tells of St. Martín's wounds. Fray Juan de Barbazán, for example, mentions: "[St. Martín] had extreme callouses on his knees from his constant praying, his sides (*ijadas*) wounded by the action of the whip, his back full of wounds by the frequent disciplines he took."

Similarly, Fray Fernando Aragones saw

said servant of God fray Martín of Porras make great and continuous penances. He wore a tunic of rough woolen cloth and a shirt of long horsehair bristles which reached down to his thighs and on the vespers of Our Lord, of Our Lady, Advent and Lent, one could see that he was suffering from the harshness of this manner of dressing. And every night about dawn in the high choir, naked, he gave himself a discipline throughout his whole body with two crude whips which lasted more than an hour.

Although the transparent message is that St. Martín is a "heroic" saint along the lines of the classical ascetic, something else is also being said. This something else begins to emerge when one notices that the majority of hurts among Indios, Negroes, mulattos, and mestizos involve wounds due to some violent encounter. St. Martín's mentor, Cirujano (Surgeon) Marcelo de Ribera, describes one of the wounded of Lima.

> Behind the false door of the convent, an Indian was stabbed in such a way that his intestines hung out. And the said servant of God fray Martín de Porras sent for this witness to cure him and not finding [St. Martín], [this witness] took care of him and put him in the infirmary with the blacks of the convent. The [friars] then went to tell the Prior how the said servant of God brought sick people from outside to cure and Indians and poor Blacks. [So] the Prior ordered said servant of God to throw out the wounded one, which then he sent to the house of his sister . . . and the next day . . . this witness having examined the Indian [again] did not find any sign of a wound except a pink stripe . . . but being well and healed the Indian went to give thanks to said servant of God.

Francisca, a black slave of the Convento, gives a similar account.

> This witness standing by the door of the house in which she lived, which is behind the said Convent of Our Lady of the Rosary, [heard] words exchanged in anger between some blacks which resulted in one of them gravely and mortally wounded with a wound in one of his flanks with his intestines hanging out. Some people seeing this [were] moved by compassion and took the wounded black to the false door of the convent so that the said venerable brother fray Martín de Porras would cure him, because he always exercised great acts of charity specially with the poor for which he felt deeply and because he was a surgeon and barber.

Anger causes wounds—at least the kind of wounds mentioned above. Anger, that sign of the irrational, is the major reason why the Indios and the Negroes of Lima were being wounded. The results of anger, moreover, can be contrasted to the results of fevers. Anger inflicts wounds from the outside. Fever inflicts itself from the inside.

The wounds of the poor of Lima, when contrasted to the fevers and ills of the friars, say something about the "outside" and "inside." The Indio and the Negro, for example, were wounded, their insides hanging out in situations that all take place outside. The ill of Lima find themselves inside. The comparison reveals what was suspected. A semiotic boundary exists that is represented by the binary opposite "outside"/"inside." Moreover, this binary opposite is associated with another binary opposite. The irrational of Lima's society are those wounded and found outside; the friars, the rational or civilized, are the ill and found inside. The net effect is a direct comparison or parallelism of the binary "irrational"/"rational" with the binary "outside"/"inside."

A reversal, however, also takes place at the same time. In the stories of the ill, the rational became irrational and found themselves inside. Furthermore, St. Martín took the irrational of Lima that were outside into the inside for healing. In doing so, St. Martín crossed an invisible boundary. The crossing was noted by the friars who complained to the prior: a code is being broken, the outside is being brought in. Thus, in the "little stories" of the wounded, the irrational of the "outside" are now brought inside. By breaking the code, St. Martín subtly reversed the meanings of "irrational"/"rational." The boundaries of Lima's social order mandated that the irrational belonged outside and the rational belonged inside. St. Martín, however, crossed those boundaries. The irrational, through St. Martín's healing, were now those on the inside.

Thus a comparison or parallelism is made and then reversed. Those who used to represent the outside—the Indios, the Negroes, the mestizo, and the mulatto—now represent the inside. The new humanity of the Americas is to be found not in rationality but in the outside. Moreover, by wounding himself, St. Martín made a deliberate connection to this new humanity. St. Martín's wounds are apparently signs of solidarity. Such solidarity, however, is a delicate matter. Lima's colonial society was hierarchical, a hierarchy strikingly paralleled in this statement by Fray Juan de Barbazán: "[This witness has a great love for St. Martín] because his experiences of so many innumerable cures as were done in his convent of this witness of religious, lay, mulatos, negros, indios, even with brute animals which always received his compassion."

This phrase is a striking parallel to the hierarchy in colonial Lima.[3] This racial/cultural/class hierarchy can also be seen as a litany of the ladder, each racial/cultural/class group corresponding to one rung on that ladder. This litany of the ladder is repeated over and over again. St. Martín's wounds connect him to this litany through the wounded ones of Lima.

Yet there is more to be said about the wounded. Another subtle but profound shift is also taking place. The "little story" of the Indio sounds remarkably the same as the "little story" of the dogs who were chased out of the Convento and ended up in Juana's house. Like the dogs of that other "little story," the Indio also ended up in Juana's house. Not all the wounded in Lima have been counted. The full meaning of St. Martín's healing cannot be reached until these other wounded—St. Martín's dogs—are counted.

THE IRRATIONAL

The "little story" by Fray Juan de Barbazán used an interesting term, *ijadas*, to describe where the wounds of St. Martín's *disciplinas* appeared. The term *ijadas* in Spanish means "side" when speaking of a human being but also means "flank" when speaking of an animal. This same term is used elsewhere in the "little stories" of the *Proceso* to describe a pain in the sides of some humans. Another consideration are the "little stories" mentioned previously in which St. Martín is called a "mulatto dog" by the friars. St. Martín, in these stories, rejoiced at being identified as a mulatto dog. This rejoicing, in a sense, is St. Martín telling the witnesses of the *Proceso,* "Yes, you're beginning to catch on. That's what I am all about." Even more interesting is the fact that the animals of the "little stories" who need St. Martín's healing suffer from wounds. Fray Hernando de Valdés gives a striking example.

> As [this witness] heard tell as an instance and an example that happened in the Great Convent of Our Lady of Rosary with a dog that belonged to father fray Juan de Vicuña, religious of said order, which had been stabbed with a sword from which blow his intestines had fallen out and dragging them went to St. Martín's cell.

The Indio, the Negro, and the dog all suffered from a wound that caused their insides to hang out. The intestines not only become a mark of solidarity but a semiotic connection. The Indio and the Negro are semiotically connected to the dog, that primal signifier of anthropological understanding. Moreover, St. Martín is now connected to all of them as well. St. Martín's wounds not only connect him to the less desirable humanity of Lima's society but also to the brute animals that inhabit the city. Continuing his work of code reversal, St. Martín healed these wounds of solidarity by putting the intestines back in, that is, by bringing the out in. Healing, that code of reordering a universe gone wrong, shows its meaning in the healing of the intestines. The way to put the universe back on track is to put what is outside back in.

What is this new order, however? The introduction of brute animals has the net effect of another subtle but more profound shift that reveals the new order that heals. The connection to the brute animals makes St. Martín more than someone identified with the outcast of Lima's society. St. Martín is now connected to brute animals, a connection that might be called a semiotic shift. This shift can be detected in these related series of "little stories." These "little stories" reveal a different version of the litany of the ladder. Fray Geronimo Baptista de Barnuy, for example, testifies:

> [he knows] that said venerable brother fray Martín de Porras was very

humble and of great charity not only with the religious, his brothers, but also with the lay and strangers, even with the animals in such a way that this witness saw that he had in his cell a dog which they had wounded and which he was healing with the same care as if he were a human person.

The lawyer Francisco Gamarra similarly testifies, "[he knows] that the said servant of God was of great charity not only with the neighbor but also with the brute animals."

This version of the ladder has two rungs, the neighbor and the animals. The space between the rungs is special. Its importance is signified in the pause one must make in describing the ladder. This pause occurs when the word "even," or "but also" separates the rest of the members of the litany from the animals. The other members of this litany are significant. They are the stranger and the neighbor. On the one hand, this special rung separates the neighbor and the animals. On the other hand, it connects them. They are disconnected by the faculty of reason (animals don't have any) but connected by St. Martín's great charity.

The pause represents a significant asymmetry, a signal that something important is taking place: a new definition of neighbor. The tension is whether to define neighbor in terms of reason or in terms of charity. Reason points to the "familiar" stranger, a neighbor, whom I call the "symmetric" Other. These strangers are like "us." Charity, however, extends to the brute, the one with the wounds, the Indios and Negroes, mulattos and mulatto dogs whom I call the "asymmetric" Other.

In a sense, the neighbor-animal dichotomy compares the binary "outside"/"inside" with the binary "asymmetric"/"symmetric." The *Proceso* is portraying here someone who does not simply follow the classical model of heroic virtue in terms of the socioeconomic poor or the outcast neighbor. The outsiders of Lima's society are more than the socioeconomic poor; they have also been connected to the asymmetric animals. Through the introduction of animals, a key semiotic progression is revealed in the *Proceso.*

The binary "irrational"/"rational" is compared through the "little stories" of the ill and the wounded with another binary "outside"/"inside." This comparison is then reversed in the breaking of the code by St. Martín, resulting in the comparison "irrational"/"rational" parallels "inside"/"outside." Thus those that are outside now belong to the "man" domain. Moreover, with the introduction of brute animals in the definition of neighbor, a new comparison is made. The binary "outside"/"inside" parallels another binary that can be characterized as "asymmetry"/"symmetry." If we put these parallelisms together with the code reversal, a new anthropology begins to emerge.

The old code of Ibero-European origin connected the man domain and the animal domain in the following way. What is irrational belongs on the outside and is considered asymmetric with respect to human being. Conversely, what is rational belongs in the inside and is considered symmetric with respect to human being. The new code of the "little stories," however, made the comparison between the binary "irrational"/"rational" and the binary "outside"/"inside" and then reversed it. What was irrational now is inside and what was rational is now outside. The parallelism between "outside"/"inside" and "asymmetric"/"symmetric," however, have not been reversed. Thus a new connection or parallelism is made. The rational—the category of the human being—is now paralleled to the asymmetric that is found outside.

The mappings of the Old World have been shifted by the humanity of the New World. The rational that maps humanity in Ibero-European anthropology is now compared to an asymmetry found outside that now maps a new humanity. This new humanity I call the asymmetric Other, human being outside the categories of the Self. The mystery of the human, then, is to be found in the crossing of true human differences. But who is this asymmetric Other? The next chapter explores this question.

7

The *Criaturas* of St. Martín

There is a popular word in the Spanish language for child. It is used mainly in the vernacular, especially by women. This word is *criatura,* which in English translates simply to "creature." It is a word of double meaning, referring both to animals and humans. It is also a word of compassion and charity. A related word, *criado,* means "servant" as well as "created." The word *crear* is etymologically related to "criar." Where the former means create, the other means to give birth as well as to nurse or take care of. Even more interesting, the words *Creador* and *Criador* are sometimes used interchangeably to refer to God.

The double and triple meanings in the word *criatura* are used in the "little stories" of the *Proceso* to reflect a boundary across time and space between the "natural" children of the Valladolid debate and the "children," or "creatures" of God. The word *criatura* in the "little stories" of St. Martín refers to some of the most marginal members of Lima's society, often women. The previous chapter saw a distinction between healing wounds and illnesses. There is, however, another kind of healing taking place in the "little stories" of the *Proceso,* the healing of something lying somewhere between a wound and illness. It is an affliction defying easy categorization yet taking in both meanings, an affliction solely belonging to women—difficult childbirth. The healing of difficult childbirth, then, takes on special significance. Like fever, difficult childbirth refers to semiotic "domains" that cross time. Difficult childbirth points to the natural child born in the debate at Valladolid. The semiotic analysis shifts here to the study of the sociohistorical dimension of the "little stories."

DIFFICULT LABOR

Semiotic domains also exist across time. This means that the signs of a cultural mosaic have a history. As history, however, they point to another time and are thus also signs. This makes it possible to study the sociohistorical dimension of a cultural mosaic. Detecting semiotic domains that cross time requires a little more effort. The method of the semiotics of culture, in this instance, attempts to find signs or metaphors that identify a historical element. The boundary between semiotic domains that encounter each other in time is also characterized by a pair of binary opposites. Such pairs of binary opposites have been mentioned before. They correspond to Gramsci's hegemony, which represented not so much a dynamic situation but a point of tension. Accommodation and resistance between dominant and subaltern groups corresponded to a pull and tug which resulted in a status quo. As such, one can expect a special type of semiotic activity near such a boundary—signs and codes that carry double meanings, one to the powerful, another to the periphery. Such double meanings involve messages of challenge and resistance. Such semiotic activity may be found in the "little stories" of difficult childbirth.

The "little stories" of St. Martín contain several accounts of the healing of difficult childbirth. Many of these "little stories" reveal class or socioeconomic emphases. Thus, "little stories" about childbirth may contain semiotic activity reflecting the presence of a "hegemonic" semiotic boundary. Clemente de Rojas, a scribe or secretary of the Crown, tells the following "little story" about the difficult childbirth of his black slave, Tomasa.

> And one occasion, which happened in the year fifty nine, this witness' black woman slave, Tomasa, while being terribly ill with a fever and during labor a terrible accident happened where the *criatura* became stuck inside the belly. And judging that there would be no way that she would live, Doña Isabel, her woman master, remembered how said servant of God had performed miracles while he had been alive and so counseled said slave to invoke together his name which they did. And at that same instant, the *criatura* returned to its place and she came out of her fever well and healthy and the next day got up.

Both fever and labor occur at the same time here and in the other "little stories" of difficult childbirth. Since fever also refers to a historical element—the epidemics in the "birth" of the New World—labor also may be a historical sign. This becomes evident as the "little story" is studied. The *criatura* of Tomasa is "stuck," even as it would have been stuck in the social polychromy of colonial Lima. The stories about childbirth carry codes of tension that contain a double meaning, one to the powerful, the other to the poor. The difficult labor of the African slave woman Tomasa, for example, meant something very different to the poor of Lima, especially the Africans, than to the powerful officials concerned with a miracle.

Tomasa's difficult labor was due to the *criatura*. This was the point of tension. Tomasa's *criatura* was stuck, even as Tomasa herself was stuck in the strictly hierarchical society of colonial Lima. Tomasa's society had been built around the category of the natural child, that category which had enslaved her and would now enslave her children. Through the healing power of St. Martín, however, Tomasa's *criatura* became unstuck and returned to its proper place. *Criaturas* were not meant to be stuck. *Criatura*, in the healing of St. Martín, became an opposing category to the natural child.

In contrast, here is another "little story" of childbirth, but this time concerning a well-respected woman of Lima, Doña Mayor Bazán de Valdés, and told by surgeon-barber Marcelo de Ribera.

> And being Doña Mayor Bazán de Valdés in difficult and painful labor, they sent for said servant of God . . . and having seen said Doña Mayor, said servant of God told her not to worry, that she would give birth to a son and that this son would give her many sorrows, and suddenly all saw that at that instant she gave birth to a son, who in his adult years, married without her consent and which was the total ruin of her family.

The title Doña is given to women of high social rank or class. Doña Valdés' experience with the miraculous intervention of St. Martín was quite different than that of Tomasa's, the African slave. St. Martín did not intervene but rather prophesied the fate of Doña Valdés' offspring. Moreover, the term *criatura* is never mentioned. Doña Valdés' child was a son, an *hijo*, one of the respected members of colonial Limean society. Unfortunately, Doña Valdés' son gave rise to the total ruin of her *casa* or family as predicted by the saintly prescience of St. Martín. Suggested here is a code of judgment against the category of child in Lima's hierarchical society. St. Martín warns, "here is what happens when a child is not born a *criatura*, but rather a child according to the categories of Lima's hierarchy." Clearly an opposition is suggested here. Doña Valdés' son is different from Tomasa's *criatura*. Doña Valdés' son is simply a child. The contrast suggests a socio-historical reference, a semiotic boundary across time. One cannot help but think of the distinction Vitoria made between the natural children of America and the normal Ibero-European children. Such elements indicate the existence of a binary opposition—"*criatura*"/ "natural child"—which suggests a semiotic boundary across time.

Another piece of evidence for this conclusion comes from another child-birth story. Doña Maria Beltran, daughter of a military officer (*alférez*), tells the following "little story."

Sixteen years ago, more or less, being in labor from four in the morning to ten at night, and seeing that I could not give birth, indeed in spite of many attempts that had been made [to make the birth possible] but because the *criatura* was stuck (*atravesada*), they had given up hope for her life and had asked her to make her confession, and even though they had put several relics of various saints on her belly, she still could not give birth, her midwife announced that the only way she could give birth is for her to be cut open and the *criatura* taken out, all immediately gasped with pain to see something so rare. But Lupercia González de Mendoza, mother of this witness, remembered she had a piece of the sleeve from the habit of the venerable servant of God fray Martín de Porras, and she took such and placed it over this witness' belly and asked fervently [of St. Martín] to intercede with his divine Majesty to give a good childbirth (*alumbramiento*). And then, on that very instant, this witness gave birth to said *criatura* alive in the presence of those there without being crippled or with any other wound so that all gave thanks to God for the mercies and favors they had received by the intercession of said venerable brother fray Martín de Porras.

Doña Maria Beltran, as the daughter of a minor police or military officer, belonged somewhere in the upper middle of colonial Lima's class structure. Her childbirth story is interesting in that it contains the term *criatura*. As such, it signals that something is being said about Vitoria's children. But exactly what? Given the presupposition of a sociohistorical encounter and the evidence so far, one would expect the term *criatura* to be used only by women of an oppressed class. Doña Maria Beltran was the wife, however, of someone who not only belonged—in subaltern terms—to the dominant or oppressor class, but as police or military officer would be instrumental in keeping the dominant class in power. This difficulty can be resolved, I believe, if one pays attention to the terms being used as well as the progression of the story.

Doña Maria's difficult childbirth was not uncommon. Difficult childbirth transcends class. Dominant and oppressed classes both were susceptible to it. Yet in the context of the *Proceso,* one expects to hear a miraculous story, a difficult childbirth miraculously about to take place. The first clue that this is not going to be like other miraculous stories is that relics of Old World saints are placed on Doña Maria's belly without any effect. The implications of this failure of Old World saints is announced by Doña Maria's midwife: Doña Maria must be cut open. All gasp at this statement. It is, indeed, very rare. Yet it is rare in two senses. The dominant class would interpret as rare that in a miraculous story, Old World saints have little if any effect on the outcome of the story. They are left contemplating a situation in which human means must be used to provide the desired outcome. For the oppressed class, however, it is rare that a member of the dominant class would find themselves in such a situation, about to be cut open or wounded. Indeed, the suggestion of cutting open Doña Maria connects this "little story" with the ones about the wounded disemboweled of the previous chapter. The suggestion of cutting open Doña Maria's belly to take out the *criatura* is, in a sense, asking the dominant class of Lima to put themselves in the place of the poor.

Moreover, Old World solutions do not work in such a reality. The gasping signals the new reality. So does the unusual word for birth, *alumbramiento,* which also means "enlightenment." A statement is about to be made which will lead to the enlightenment of the people surrounding Doña Maria's bed. It is a story meant for them, the dominant class of Limean society. As the story unfolds, it is the relic of a would-be New World saint, a saint that is yet-to-be, that has effect. Old-World-saints-that-are are pitted against a New-World-saint-to-be, the result being a perfect *criatura* without blemish or wounds. The nature of the semiotic challenge then becomes apparent. The New-World-saint-to-be is the answer to the mysterious conflict occasioned by stuck *criaturas.* The solution to Lima's class conflict is not Old World solutions applied to *criaturas.* This is, in a sense, what Vitoria had attempted. Nor are we left with conventional solutions that are drastic and violent. The solution lies in New World approaches, in a New World humanity that is having a difficult birth. With the aid, however, of St. Martín, this New World humanity, this New World *criatura* will be different from the *criatura* envisioned by the Old World. The New World *criatura* will be healthy.

In the tales of a miraculous childbirth, the Procurator in Rome may have seen a miracle, but the *criaturas* of Lima saw a hierarchy dismantled. Such are the double meanings characteristic of hegemonic semiotic boundaries across time. Moreover, in the official recognition of the miraculous childbirth of the African slave woman Tomasa lay the necessary admission that the children born from natural children merited the miraculous intervention of God. Such concessions reflect the nature of the semiotic activity referring to sociohistorical encounters. The culprit was the imperfect *criatura* of Vitoria, the natural child stuck in the birth of a New World mired in Old World understandings. St. Martín's *criatura,* unlike Vitoria's natural child, is meant to be an alumbramiento rather than a darkness. These childbirth stories thus reveal a binary opposition across time: "*criatura*"/"natural child." The healing of St. Martín suggests that this binary opposition is about to be transformed, a boundary is about to be crossed. The next step is to look for signs of such transformation.

OTHER *CRIATURAS*

There are other stories of *criaturas* in the "little stories" of St. Martín. Fray Antonio Gutiérrez tells the following story about another type of *criatura.*

A few days before said venerable brother fray Martín de Porras died, he told this witness while in his deathbed, since this witness was his nurse, that he would die of this disease. Nonetheless, the doctor would keep prescribing a certain medicine which meant killing a certain number of animals such as puppies, doves, and chickens, and [St. Martín] took this killing to heart and he heard said venerable brother fray Martín de Porras ask why were they killing those creatures of God (*criaturas de Dios*) since it would be God's will that he would die this way and so it happened that he died of this disease.

To heal the healer, animals were to be killed. Yet St. Martín had always healed animals. Such is the irony expressed in this "little story." With reference to this irony, St. Martín calls the animals to be sacrificed for his health creatures of God. The term emphasizes that these animals point ultimately to God, and just as God was in charge of their life, so was God in charge of St. Martín's life. Both the animals and St. Martín share something in common: they are creatures of God. Another story about *criaturas* is told by Fray Antonio Gutiérrez.

On one occasion, this witness remembers that having found in the barn where mules are kept (*muladar*), a mule that had broken a leg, and was so wounded that it was hopeless, said venerable brother fray Martín de Porres cured her saying: "*Criatura* of God, heal." And in a few days said mule was healthy and cured.

It is appropriate that a mulatto would cure this mula, for both shared a common name and a common hopelessness. This hopelessness turned to healing when the mule was transformed from mula to creature of God. The effect is instantaneous in English or Spanish. The mule immediately takes on a certain dignity and bearing when it is being referred to as a creature of God. This was the healing phrase. It was also a challenge to a social order built on the exploitation of natural children. By healing animals and calling them *criaturas,* St. Martín expanded the meaning of the words *child* and *natural* in unexpected and striking ways, transforming the meanings into an assertion that not even the powerful could deny. Moreover, the identification of St. Martín as a creature of God gives an important clue about the transformations taking place.

Further evidence for this conclusion comes from the following story by Fray Juan Vazquez de Parra, St. Martín's young apprentice.

On the eve of the feast of the Holy Spirit, he would as great devotion borrow two hair shirts from Castile from the businesses along the street. . . . One of the hair shirts was for P. fray Juan Masias, his companion and friend. . . . Together, they would go to the banana plantation in the garden of the Recollects, where they would pray throughout the entire eve giving themselves great disciplines and their backs would be filled with welts. Later he would come to me, Juan Vasquez, to be healed. I would say to him "Father, what is there to cure because this is not due to the bad work of the whip but to those mosquitos that are here? Let's go to our convent where there are no mosquitos." The servant of God responded: "How are we to look before God, if we do not give food to the hungry?" I said to him: "Father, these, are they people? Aren't they little animals?" "Nonetheless," he said, "they ought to be fed for they are *criaturas de Dios,* now wash me."

St. Martín's insistence that it was not the mosquitos but the whip that had wounded him signals a sociohistorical encounter. Vazquez' question is odd. Mosquito bites hardly compare with welts from a whip. Vazquez' analysis of St. Martín's infliction seems almost comical, and it is meant to be. This "little story" makes fun of those who see the suffering and hunger around them and believe it is due to the natural way of things rather than inflicted, to mosquito bites rather than the cruel bite of the whip. Vazquez' question, "are they people?" was the anthropological question of the Valladolid debate. St. Martín's answer, "they are *criaturas de Dios,*" is the anthropological answer given by the new humanity of the Americas. It was not an expected answer. It brings the meaning of human being into the meanings of *criatura* and combines them in unexpected and marvelous ways. There is another clue, however, to the nature of the transformation taking place. The mosquitos, says St. Martín, ought to be fed because they are *criaturas de Dios.* The connection between *criaturas* and feeding suggests a further transformation.

A CREATURELY SACRAMENT

The theology of sacraments depends naturally on a theology of human being. Both depend on the question of grace. It is not surprising, then, to learn that one of the most debated issues in the New World was whether Amerindians, Africans, mulattos, and mestizos, all natural children, were capable of receiving the Eucharist. The consequences of this debate have already been outlined in a previous chapter. Such an important sociohistorical encounter resulted in great semiotic activity in our cultural mosaic through "little stories" that refer to the sacrament in some way.

A recurring set of "little stories," for example, refers to St. Martín's love of the Eucharist. Central to these stories is the strange disappearance of St. Martín when he receives the sacrament of the Holy Eucharist. One such "little story" has already been told in a previous chapter, the "little story" concerning the Archbishop of Mexico who sent for St. Martín. He could not be found because he had disappeared after taking communion. As mentioned previously, this "little story" points to a sociohistorical encounter, a challenge being articulated. The stories of the sacrament of Eucharist involve semiotic domains that exist across time and about which one can expect great semiotic activity. Such activity may be found in this story by Francisco Perez Quintero, the master carpenter of the Convento.

> And that this witness was told by a religious of said order named fray Tomás Román . . . how the said venerable brother fray Martín de Porras, the day in which he received the most holy Sacrament, he would disappear and hide in said convent in such a way that he would not be found. And this witness knows and experienced that in the day that said servant of God communed, it was a constant that although they looked for him all over the convent but he did not appear by any means because he hid himself in such a way that he could not be found.

There are many more accounts of a similar nature: when St. Martín communes, St. Martín disappears. By his absence, St. Martín is apparently being connected to the sacrament. The meaning of this connection suggests itself when Aquinas' writings, which are the object of study for most Dominicans and thus would be very familiar to the friars of the Convento, are examined. Aquinas (1964, III, q.61, ad 1), for example, says this about the sacraments:

> The sacraments are necessary for man's salvation for three reasons. The first is taken from the way in which humanity naturally functions in achieving knowledge of spiritual or intelligible realities. . . . The second reason is taken from man's own state. For by sinning, he incurred an affection for physical things and so made himself subject to them. Now the remedy designed to heal man has to be applied to that part of his nature affected by the sickness. Hence it was appropriate for God to apply spiritual medicine to men by means of certain physical signs.

and

> medicine is not necessary unless we are sick, as we are told in Matthew, *those who are well have no need of a physician*. Now, the sacraments are, in a certain sense, spiritual medicines (*spirituales medicinae*) applied as remedies against the wounds of sin (*contra vulnera peccati*). (1964, III, q.61, ad 2)

These descriptions by Aquinas would have been well known to the friars and those they instructed in catechism. If St. Martín can be compared to a sacrament, then his *disciplinas* take on new meaning. St. Martín becomes a tangible sign of some spiritual reality. As such, St. Martín is also a healing remedy for "the healing of wounds inflicted by sin." St. Martín's wounds are signs of another reality, a violent one in which wounds are being inflicted by some great sin. Not mosquito bites, but welts from a whip are the focus of St. Martín's penitential practices. Through the whip, Martín calls attention to the violent nature of the sin operating in Lima. The feeding of the mosquitos with his own blood connects St. Martín's sacramental nature with the sacrament of the Eucharist.

The Eucharist, in the Scholastic system of Ibero-European theology, had additional meanings besides that of healing. St. Thomas saw the Eucharist as *spirituale alimentum* (1964, III, q.73, ad 1) (spiritual food) which signifies *communio* or *amicitia* or *unitas* (communion, fellowship, or unity), *sacrificium* (sacrifice), and *viaticum respectu futuri*, which may be translated as "provisions for the journey in light of the future" (1964, III, q.73, ad 4). St. Martín's disappearance after communion also ties him to these meanings. The meaning of Eucharist as sacrifice, for example, is also signified in St. Martín's sacrificial practice of the disciplines which, in turn, creates his wounds which, in turn, signify a solidarity, communion, fellowship with the poor of Lima, and, of course, with the animals.

"Little stories" that refer implicitly to the Eucharist are many and varied. Fray Fernando Aragones tells the following story.

> And around noon, about the time to eat, the said servant of God went to the refectory and took a cup and a bowl to collect any food left from the religious who ate by his side. If he saw any poor at the door of the refectory his impatience was notable until he was able to bring them food, and in having met their need, he calmed down and ate but bread and water so that through his great abstinence more could be fed, a sign of his great charity. And after having finished eating he took his bowl and his cup full of food and went to the kitchen of the infirmary where he waited on sick and impoverished Spanish, Blacks, Indians and the poor from the neighborhood and dogs and cats which at that hour waited for sustenance from the hand of the said servant of God. And before distributing the food he would give them a blessing saying: "May God increase it through his infinite mercy." And it seems that that is what happened, that God increased the food through [St. Martín's] hand for all ate and their bowls were filled outside and all were contented, even the dogs and cats.

St. Martín, like a priest about to celebrate the Eucharist, carries bowl and cup to commune the poor, the Indio, the Negro, the mulatto, and the mestizo. This communion takes place outside with food brought from the inside. The theologians may have debated about the capacity of the human beings standing at the kitchen door of the Convento to receive the Eucharist, but St.

Martín has no doubts. What is more striking (but not unexpected) is that dogs and cats are also communed. This is not so much a code reversal as it is a subtle challenge. The act of communion is an act of fellowship. St. Martín carries the fellowship of the refectory with his brother monks out to the kitchen where he continues the fellowship with the poor and the animals. Such fellowship is problematic. According to St. Thomas (1964, III, q.25, art.4): "no irrational creature can be loved out of charity; and for three reasons. Two of these reasons refer in a general way to friendship [or fellowship, *amicitas*], which cannot have an irrational creature for its object."

Yet St. Martín most definitely is portrayed as having irrational creatures as object of his charity. One wonders at the chutzpah of the witnesses of the *Proceso*. As anxious as they were to have their "saint" officially recognized, they kept introducing definite challenges to the professional theologians who would dutifully pore over the depositions of the process. The most reasonable conclusion is that the witnesses were challenging a theology or a theological anthropology that had social and political consequences. St. Martín's sacramental behavior carries rational humans across the boundary that separates rational human beings from the world of irrational creatures. A theological understanding of human being that has reason as the *sine qua non* of human nature is being challenged and an alternative suggested.

St. Martín's contemporary biographer allows us a glimpse into the alternative anthropology being suggested (de Medina 1964, 94).

> It is true that charity does not oblige us to love irrational ones, because attributing to God this virtue and, thus, through God to the rational, the brutes having no reason do not communicate intellectually with man, and because of this one need not love them out of charity, and also because this is founded on the beatitude of loving the neighbor which [the brutes] are also incapable of. Yet, St. Thomas still says, a man of charity can love the brute attributing to God that love, *as creature (criadura) to Creator (Criador),* taking joy in the conservation of animals for the honor of God and for the use of the neighbor. It is thus that the venerable servant of God Fray Martín de Porras loved the brutes, as *criaturas de Dios,* calling them his brothers through Creation. (emphasis mine)

If we contrast this explanation with Vitoria's justification for the conquest, one sees what the semiotic challenge is about. The ultimate mystery of human being is not so much reason but that the human is a creature of God. What is human cannot be known without reference to God, and that reference lies not with the distinctiveness of the human but with the connectedness of creation. This I call the anthropology of creatureliness, and it puts the mystery of human being on the wonder and power and novelty of God's creative activity expressed in the works of his Creation. When the anthropology of creatureliness is examined, all the justification for the exploitation of America's natural wealth, material, irrational, and rational, is undermined and dismantled.

The anthropology of creatureliness perhaps reaches its most explicit articulation in the following "little story" by Fray Fernando Aragones, which has already been told. Because of its importance, I repeat it once more.

> And it was the case that in a basement that was below the infirmary of the convent that a female dog and cat ended up. And fearing that mothers and children would die of hunger, he brought every day to bring them a bowl of soup, and while they ate he would say: "Eat, be quiet, and don't quarrel." And thus, it seemed, they would obey him … and one day it happened that a mouse came out to eat from the same plate, and when said servant of God saw him, he told him: "Brother, don't bother the little ones, go for it and eat and leave with God." And so it happened that neither the mouse nor the puppies, nor the kittens, were bothered and all ate in peace.

This striking image of dogs, cats, and mice drinking peacefully from the same bowl of soup at the feet of the mulatto St. Martín de Porres is representative of the eucharistic images concerning St. Martín. The challenging yet visionary meaning was transparent to the people of St. Martín's day. Medina's biographer describes it (de Medina 1964, 98-99).

> And thus [with this sight] it seemed God wanted to honor his servant with the prowess prophesied of his first coming by the prophet Isaias [Isa. 11:6] who told of the coming together of many definite brutes, the wolf and the lamb, and the goat with the leopard (*pardo*); for here the same fellowship took place, if not goat and irrational leopard (*pardo irracional*), at least dogs, cats, and mouse, by virtue of a rational Mulato (*Pardo racional*), who was the same Fray Martín. (emphasis mine)

Medina's pun on the word *pardo*, which means both leopard and mulatto, contrasts the rational with the irrational even as it brings them together in the understanding of human being represented by St. Martín. This understanding surfaces in the dog, cat, and mouse story mentioned above. This "little story" envisions a cosmic and sacramental fellowship. As such, this "little story" is a reference to the end times such as the one envisioned by Isaiah.

> The wolf shall live with the lamb,
> the leopard shall lie down with the kid,
> the calf and the lion and the fatling together,
> and a little child shall lead them.

Crossing wild and domestic boundaries

Isaiah's vision crossed the boundaries between wild and domestic animals—a lion and a lamb, a wolf and a kid—to envision an end time when the wilderness would be one with the civilized. The "little stories" of St. Martín, on the other hand, envision an end time when the boundaries crossed are between domestic animals. In other words, within the civilized existed a wilderness, a boundary where some human beings were considered natural and others civilized. At the feet of the little child, St. Martín, these boundaries are now crossed, presenting an image of hope for the future of the people of the New World.

Yet such an image is not simply for the end times. Theresa of Avila once said, "All the way to heaven is heaven." Such is also the meaning of the dog, cat, and mouse story. This "little story" is also a viaticum. It is not only a vision of what heaven will look like but also provision for the journey there. The road to heaven shall be a sacramental fellowship that embraces the cosmos. We are to be sacraments to one another and to the cosmos.

The Eucharist, for example, is now presented as being shared by rational and irrational *criaturas.* No additional rungs in the hierarchy of being are being constructed, for none are needed. It is not the hierarchy of being that is at fault, but the demon of rationality presented as a crucial rung defining humanity. St. Martín's anthropology refers to the entire hierarchy of being. This does not avoid the question of distinguishing the human from other *criaturas,* for it points clearly to the elements that must be taken into account to define humanity.

These elements are to be found in the hierarchy of being as being composed as a sacramental fellowship (not exploitation) of asymmetric (truly different) *criaturas.* As such, the hierarchy of being is not so much a vertical ladder as a cosmic fellowship made possible by the human *criatura.* Human beings are as different from one another as a dog is from a cat or a cat from a mouse. Nonetheless, human beings have the capacity to cross these differences so they may drink from the same bowl of soup. This capacity is the distinguishing characteristic of humanity as articulated in the "little stories" of St. Martín and is the topic of the next chapter.

Cosmic fellowship

8

The Anthropology of Creatureliness

Second only to the Virgin of Guadalupe, St. Martín de Porres enjoys great respect and devotion among Latin Americans. The reason for this popularity has been seen by many as either the manipulation of the masses by the powerful or syncretism at work in a New World Christianity that never matured. I offer a third reason. St. Martín's popularity is due to his ability to interpret the faith of many who face insuperable challenges and in doing so allowing that faith to be appropriated as one's own. This interpretation does not take place at the level of scholarly discourse in a university hall but at the level of signs, codes, and messages in a cultural mosaic. As such, St. Martín is known through his "little stories," many of which have been told in this work. These "little stories," in turn, open up a world of profound meaning in which the "Big Story" is found. It is this "Big Story" which, in the end, allows the popular to interpret their challenged faith. St. Martín knows something about the human condition. People come to St. Martín to learn about the "Big Story" of their lives and in doing so find or renew their faith.

The "Big Story" of St. Martín, however, is different from a previous "Big Story" about human being. The "Big Story" that led to the cultural mosaic of colonial Lima could be found in the important anthropological debate of Valladolid in 1550, which I will review briefly. The debate was occasioned by the papal bulls of donation that granted the newly discovered lands to the Crown of Castile. The encounter with the "primitive" Amerindians of the Caribbean led to the quasi-institution of the Encomienda, an institution meant to take care of these "primitives," for they apparently could not take care of themselves. The Encomienda, however, became an institution of abuse and slavery of the Amerindian. The discovery by Cortez and Pizarro of the "advanced" Amerindian, the Aztec and Inca, people who without a doubt knew how to govern themselves, brought the entire issue of donation and the

abuses of the Encomienda to a crisis. The lack of medieval categories for the
Amerindian prevented a legal solution. The political issue of conquest led to
a search for a new anthropology. This new anthropology was the subject of
the Valladolid debate and hinged on the acknowledgment of true human
difference, the "asymmetry" of the human condition.

The new anthropology was discussed from three perspectives. The majority perspective represented by the jurist Ginés de Sepúlveda argued that
the Amerindians were homunculi, little less than human. In effect, this
perspective avoided the anthropological issue by denying true humanity to
the Amerindian. The minority perspective represented by Bartolomé de las
Casas argued that the Amerindians were barbarians secundum quid, symmetric others whose differences were superficial rather than fundamental. This
perspective, in effect, avoided the issue of true human differences. The
moderate perspective represented by Vitoria and the Salamanca School
argued that the Amerindian was a natural child with a mind *in potentia*. I
believe this perspective correctly confronted the issue of true human difference raised by the Amerindian. It did so by creating a new category in the
hierarchy of being—the natural child. Meant to protect the Amerindian,
Vitoria's argument played into the hands of those who wanted to continue
the profitable exploitation of the Amerindian through the Encomienda. The
Encomienda, after all, was an institution for natural children, a school where
children could be taught to be adults. The Crown, then, had every right to
take over the lands of these natural children so they might be educated. The
political question of conquest was answered not through the resolution of a
legal issue but through the modification of an old anthropology.

Vitoria had surmised correctly that true difference was the issue at the
heart of the encounter with the Amerindian but, unfortunately, had not gone
far enough in his anthropological solution. His category of natural children,
instead of leading to the protection of the Amerindian, allowed the continuation of the Encomienda with the resultant demographic collapse of the
Amerindian. The commencement of the Atlantic slave trade coincided with
this demographic collapse. The category of natural child was now applied to
the recently discovered sub-Saharan Africans as justification for their en-
slavement.

The issue remained under the surface, for the emerging colonial society
of the Americas depended on a strong social hierarchy for its existence, a
social hierarchy informed by Vitoria's natural child. Nonetheless, Vitoria did
not foresee the great mixing of races in the Americas. What, after all, was
the product of a sub-Saharan African natural child and an Ibero-European
adult? The categories the Old World had made to govern and make sense of
the New World broke down with the mestizos and mulattos of America. The
symptoms of this breakdown can be found in the "little stories" of the
beatification process of the mulatto St. Martín. There Vitoria's category of
natural child is challenged with an alternative category: the *criatura de Dios*.

The nature of the *criatura* is revealed in the cosmic eucharistic-like fellowship provided by St. Martín. The *criatura de Dios* is not some rung in a cosmic ladder but part of a cosmic fellowship. True human differences are not variations along a vertical scale of value but elements of a horizontal fellowship of sacramental grace. This I call the anthropology of creatureliness.

THE NEW WORLD "BIG STORY"

The Old World "Big Story" centered around reason. Reason distinguished the human being from the animals. Unfortunately, in the violent and unequal encounter with America, reason was also used to distinguish the powerful from the less powerful, the civilized adult from the natural child. The "little stories" of St. Martín offer an alternative. The human being is the asymmetric other who defies easy identification or categorizing. In other words, there exist true differences among human beings. This means that each human being is so unique that the Creator can call this creature by his or her own personal name. The human is one-of-a-kind, at least with respect to his or her Creator, yet longs for a life in common with others.[1] Humans have the need and the capacity for fellowship. These are the two principal messages communicated by the "little stories" of St. Martín. As such, they present a paradoxical situation that points to a "Big Story." Human creatures are uniquely different yet were created for fellowship across those differences.

The "little stories" address this paradox through the dog stories, the stories of St. Martín healing dogs as if they were people. By healing dogs as if they were people, St. Martín points to the key that solves the paradox. Although humans are one of a kind, one thing can be said about all humans: they are creatures of God. The human creature, however, is special among the other creatures. Only one-of-a-kind creatures can know themselves as "I." This, in turn, makes it possible for this very special creature to know "Thou," their Creator. As such, the New World "Big Story" is not really new at all. It is the old "Big Story" of the Church's tradition whose meaning has now become clearer.

The old "Big Story" may be characterized briefly: human creatures were created to know and love God. The traditional name for this relationship is the imago Dei, the image of God. Human creatures were created in the image of God, which gives them the capacity to know and love God. Knowing and loving God are the two elements of the Church's traditional "Big Story" that must be kept in balance. Yet the Ibero-European emphasis on reason had created an imbalance. St. Martín's charity toward irrational dogs points out that the Old World category of reason emphasized the "know" part of the traditional "Big Story" over the "love" component. This had the effect of narrowing the full meaning of human. Love, after all, in the traditional "Big

Story," leads to fellowship. The love component of the traditional "Big Story" means that human creatures not only have the capacity to know God but also to have fellowship with their Creator. By emphasizing knowing over loving in the meaning of human, the Ibero-European sense of the "Big Story" had undermined the fellowship dimension of the human creature. St. Martín, by forming fellowship with all sorts of nonhuman creatures, kept emphasizing this dimension.

The healing of dogs as if they were people, for example, pointed out what is at stake in loving God and having fellowship with one's Creator. One must cross the gap of asymmetry inherent in the created order. God created the world in marvelous diversity, a garden of fecund asymmetries.[2] No greater difference exists, however, among these marvelous asymmetries than that between the Creator and the one-of-a-kind human creature, yet this fundamental asymmetry must be crossed if the human creature is to love and form fellowship with his or her Creator. The issue of identity is crucial to the crossing of this fundamental gap.

Nonhuman creatures, for example, do not know who they are. Their identity is hidden from them not so much because they are irrational (actually many nonhuman creatures are capable of some type of reasoning) but because it is given to them. In other words, nonhuman creatures have no way to bridge the ultimate asymmetry between themselves and their Creator. They simply participate in what they are. Human creatures, on the other hand, possess a very special difference. The human creatures' one-of-a-kind-"ness" makes their creaturely identity problematic. Human creatures do not have an identity given to them; they must find it.[3] One-of-a-kind creatures have no categories by which to know who they are. This gives the human, however, a freedom nonhuman creatures can never know. Human creatures are truly free. They are free to cross boundaries of identity, even the seemingly insuperable boundary of self-identity. As such, the human, the one-of-a-kind creature, is free to make relationships where none existed before. St. Martín, for example, demonstrated his extraordinary freedom by the ease with which he crossed the human boundaries of Lima's colonial hierarchy as well as in his special relationship to animals. This ability to cross boundaries makes possible human fellowship with the Creator.

Humans, however, are also free to deny their special relationship with the Creator. Human creatures are free to deny their one-of-a-kind-"ness." The asymmetric other under these conditions becomes a symmetric self, no longer looking for identity as a one-of-a-kind creature but defining an artificial identity for itself. The encomenderos did just that in the violent and unequal encounter of Ibero-Europe and America. They denied the Amerindian their human differences. The encomenderos did this by defining an artificial identity for themselves (the civilized adult) that led to the exploitation and slavery of millions (the natural children).

Ultimately, sin in the Anthropology of Creatureliness is an act of symmetry, of *subsuming differences for the goals of a personal freedom*. The subsuming of differences under the conditions of symmetry is ultimately a violent act, an act against the cosmic order which was created not so much as a hierarchy but as a fecundity of different creatures. An attempt to diminish or compromise that fecundity is to go against the intention of the Creator for Creation. Sin, in the anthropology of creatureliness, is an act that is at once personal and social. It is personal, for in denying that God made and knows one's self as one-of-a-kind, the symmetric self sins against his or her own humanity. It is also social, for in order to subsume differences, the symmetric self must force other human creatures who are one-of-a kind to their Creator to become artificially (and forcefully) symmetric to the self who now usurps the relationship with the Creator.

Although human creatures can sin by destroying fellowship, this was not the original intention. We were meant to take part in the creatureliness of Creation, not to diminish it. The "little stories" made the strong point that we are born *criaturas*. But we are *criaturas* made in the image of the Creator. As such, human beings participate in their own creatureliness. We are, as Philip Hefner (1993), the director of the Chicago Center for Science and Religion, says, co-creators with God. The ability of human creatures to participate in their own creatureliness, to be co-creators with God, is crucial in forming fellowship because human fellowship is, in a sense, an act of creation. The act of entering a relationship where one knows and loves the other also means that one is known and loved by an other. I love my wife, Kathryn. I am also loved by her. Such love, at its best, means two separate freedoms becoming one. Two creatures sharing one freedom means participating in each other's creatureliness, each other's identity. When this happens, I come to know who I am because of who she is. This means that when a human creature engages in fellowship with an other, he or she encounters his or her own identity in the image of God carried by the other. As such, both one-of-a-kind creatures share in each other's image of God. This means that our one-of-a-kind-"ness" has been altered. One's image of God is now also informed by an other's imago Dei, and we become a new creature. To participate in fellowship is to be "re-created," to be recreated.

The image of God is not some static stamp that acts like a cookie cutter stamping out identical human beings but a dynamic force that continually shapes the human creature. Thus the image of God calls the human creature into fellowship. In doing so, the human creature participates in his or her creatureliness, entering into the very process of creation which the Creator graciously has offered to share with this very special creature. The ability to participate in our own creatureliness is to participate in the creatureliness of the cosmos. Nothing represents our created goal to have fellowship with the Creator more than participating in a fellowship that includes the Creation. This is suggested in the "little story" of the dog, the cat, and the mouse.

The dog, the cat, and the mouse are not the only creatures sharing fellowship around a bowl of soup. Another creature is also with them: the creature of God who is St. Martín. As such, the dog, the cat, and the mouse story reveals the creatureliness of the human, an identity found through the capacity for cosmic fellowship given the human creature by the Creator. By participating in the creatureliness of each other and of the cosmos, the human creature discovers who he or she is, because the Creator of the human creature is also the One who created the cosmos.

The cosmic fellowship depicted in the dog, cat, and mouse story, however, also reveals a re-creaturing of the Creation. The creatureliness of dog, cat, and mouse in the story had been transformed through one human creature's charitable search for identity. St. Martín, through his great charity for the dogs, cats, and mice of Lima, had transformed natural enemies into natural fellows. Asymmetric boundaries had been crossed and a new creatureliness achieved. Creatureliness and identity had been transformed and interrelated in the cosmic fellowship enabled by St. Martín. The dog, cat, and mouse story may be an eschatological image, an image of the end times, but it is also an image of what the journey to the end time will look like. The road to heaven will be found through the charitable search for human identity.

THE IMAGINATION

A problem remains. The "little stories" of St. Martín protest the category of reason as used by the Ibero-European in defining the distinctiveness of human beings. Does this mean that the "little stories" meant to get rid of the category of reason altogether? I do not believe so. I believe that the "little stories" aimed at expanding our understanding of reason. The protest was not the category itself but the narrowness of it. The *criaturas* of St. Martín being "stuck" at birth did not represent Lima's society *per se,* but the narrowness of it. Something similar can be said for the Ibero-European category of reason. Reason, in the Ibero-European sense, narrowed the full meaning of human reasoning. I believe that the "little stories" meant to expand that narrowness with a larger category—the imagination.

The imagination has been considered a necessary evil in the theological and philosophical tradition.[4] Augustine saw the imagination as the "humble servant of a higher intellect." Richard of St. Victor compared the imagination and contemplation: the imagination is to contemplation as a maid, representing the outer room of bodily desires, is to her mistress, representing the inner sanctuary of reason. Aquinas compared the imagination to a storehouse: images received through the senses are retained and preserved by the imagination, which becomes a storehouse of forms received through the senses. The imagination, then, in its various guises has a recurring theme. It is the intermediary that connects the sensible world of Creation and the rational world of the soul. Yet the imagination has had an ambivalent place in the western tradition. It is at once despised but claimed essential for knowing. The "little stories," I believe, address this ambivalence and challenge the presumed relationship between reason and the imagination. It is reason which is the servant of the imagination and not the other way around. This makes the imagination a more fundamental category than reason. Reason is, in effect, but one aspect of the imagination.

This can be seen clearly in the natural sciences. Amos Funkestein (1986) demonstrated the crucial role between the facts of natural science and the scientific imagination. The modern scientific view of motion, for example, could not have been possible without taking the imagination seriously. Aristotelian physics assumed that objects came to rest when their "motive" force ceased. This is also our intuitive conclusion. All of us know that when we kick or throw a ball it will eventually stop rolling. Modern physics, however, believes that this is not the nature of things. Where no friction exists, a ball when kicked or thrown will tend to keep moving. This is known as the principle of inertia. This principle, however, was not a product of reason itself but reason in service of the scientific imagination. What is striking is that this product of the imagination was confirmed when the first human beings went into space and performed the experiment. The imagination had been more powerful than an act of reason by itself! (*See* García-Rivera 1994a, 51-59.) The principle of inertia established the crucial nature of the imagination in understanding the sensible. Modern science, then, may be characterized by this "paradoxical mediation between the factual and imaginary" (Funkestein 1986). This kind of mediation, however, does not do away with reason but rather puts it in its true place as the servant of the imagination.

The scientific imagination is similar if not identical to the religious imagination that generated the "little stories." Another name for the "Big Story" in religious studies is myth. A scholar who discusses the role of the imagination in the "Big Story" is Lawrence Sullivan. In his ground-breaking work, *Icanchu's Drum* (1988), Sullivan saw the "Big Story," or myth, not as a type of narrative but as a "quality of imaginal existence." Sullivan, in fact, sees the "Big Story" as "the imagination beholding its own reality and plumbing the sources of its own creativity as it relates to creativity in every form (plant and planetary life, animal fertility, intelligence, art)" (22).

Thus, the "Big Story" reveals the imagination itself. Sullivan's findings imply that knowing and loving are related in their most profound sense through the imagination. To know something or somebody is to include that something or somebody into one's own world, one's "imaginal existence." Such imaginal existence, however, does not mean existing in a subjective world known only to that individual. Rather it means existing in a world in which relationships with very real creatures are made possible through the imagination. Human creatures, if they are to survive, must make their way in this world by knowing it in a very real sense. How does the human creature know, for example, that a given tree will yield edible fruit three months from now? This knowledge is not the result of immediate experience or simply of cold, logical reason, but an act of imaginal existence. The imagination enables the human creature to survive and exist in the world.

Yet more is at stake. The human creature is not the only one that participates in imaginal existence. Other creatures, after all, must also know their world in other to survive. This knowledge has been given to them by their Creator. This means that nonhuman creatures also live an imaginal existence that knows the relationships they have with other creatures, but they do so through the imagination of their Creator. Thus, in the imaginal existence of the creatures of Creation, one may find the imagination of God. What is at stake for the human creature is participation in the imagination of the Creator. This can only happen through cosmic fellowship. An imaginal existence that includes a cosmic fellowship brings to fruition the human capacity to know and love God. In engaging his or her imagination with the imagination of the Creator, a new, or rather original imaginal existence becomes a reality.[5] This original "imaginal existence" is nothing less than the existence which the imagination of the traditional "Big Story" compels us to explore.[6]

The dog, cat, and mouse drinking from the same bowl of soup at the feet of St. Martín represents this imaginal existence. This "little story," however, also points to a New World understanding of grace. Grace's most profound meaning is not redemption but healing in the cosmic sense.[7] Grace, after all, names a special relationship with God. This relationship, in recent times, has been understood in a very narrow sense to refer to the redemption of the human creature by God. Although it certainly means that, grace also refers to the relationship the Creator has with all Creation. To separate redemption from creation leaves the goal of redemption, the recreation of the human creature, empty. God redeems us as the Maker and Sustainer of all creatures and the cosmic order of things. Yet in recent times, the God-relation to the cosmos has become separated from the God-relation to the human creature. The former is the starting point for theologies of Creation, the latter for theologies of the human. The "little stories" of St. Martín reveal that separating the God-relation is a symptom of the Ibero-European ladder of being.

Sin in the "little stories" was caused by a demon on a ladder that was responsible for artificial and unnatural relationships in Lima's society. These artificial and unnatural relationships extended to the creatures of the "little stories." Through his healing, St. Martín restored the original relationships the Creator had intended for the creatures of Lima, human and nonhuman. Healing refers to setting things right, to bringing order back to a chaotic universe. Healing, in this cosmic sense, expands a narrowed view of redemption. Redemption is a cosmic healing recreating the human creature. The redemption of the human creature also heals the cosmic order. Thus grace restores the God-relation, the relation of the human creature with his or her

Creator which, in the most profound sense, is an act of healing that restores the God-relation to the entire cosmos. Thus the New World understanding of grace does not split the God-relation into a God-relation with the human creature and a God-relation with the Creation. Instead it asks us to imagine ourselves as creatures of God, as St. Martín did, in order to imagine the act of grace, the act of restoring the original order of Creation into which chaos had entered through human sin.

St. Martín's anthropology of creatureliness was not so much a dismantling of the hierarchy of being but a protest that the metaphor of a ladder with a special rung of rationality where the human stood was not only inappropriate but dangerous. St. Martín did not see the elements of a hierarchy of being as rungs but as asymmetric relationships that required the imagination of the Creator for their possibility. The hierarchy of being was not so much a ladder as it was a quality of imaginal existence, a fellowship of grace. The experience of grace, of healing in the cosmic sense, was an experience of being a *criatura de Dios,* sustained by and sustaining a gracious living imagination pointing to the source of our identity, the meaning of our asymmetry, the Creador-Criador, the Maker and Sustainer of life and the world.

If anything, the "little stories" of St. Martín have shown how popular religion engages this original imaginal existence that reveals the imagination of the Creator. If, in modern centuries, popular religion has been disdained by specialists in the academy or the Church, it is because of a failure of the specialist's imagination. Moreover, the "little stories" have shown that part of our spiritual malaise today is due to a failure of the imagination. The "Big Story" of the Church's tradition has much broader and expansive categories by which to engage this world than are articulated by our society. The "Big Story" of the Church's tradition offers us full life, not as the narrow rational beings of the encomenderos that live in a tiny universe created through forced human relationships, but as *criaturas de Dios* that live in the expansive universe of cosmic fellowship. As guide and sacrament, St. Martín shows us how to enter into the Church's imagination through his "little stories" so that we, too, in making them our own, may become like him, a creature of God.

Notes

1. A MYSTERY IN LIMA

1. This "little story," like all the "little stories" about to be told, is found in Secretariado Martín de Porres (1960), which I will refer to simply as the *Proceso*. The *Proceso* contains the eyewitness depositions given at the beatification process of St. Martín over the years 1660 to 1671. Each "little story" will be referenced only by the eyewitness who told it.

2. *Hidalgo* is a contraction of "hijo de algo" or "son of somebody," which denotes a person of noble class but without property or land.

3. The earliest sources spell Don Juan's last name Porras, yet somehow the name eventually came to be spelled Porres. In the "little stories," St. Martín is referred to as Martín de Porras, even though he is known throughout the Latin American world as San Martín de Porres. I shall refer to San Martín de Porres as St. Martín. This Mestizaje of languages, I think, would have been pleasing to him.

4. Many biographies have been written about St. Martín. The most important one is by Fray Bernardo de Medina, O.P. Medina was one of the witnesses who testified before the Apostolic Commission gathering data for St. Martín's beatification. Medina was also St. Martín's first biographer. Medina was urged a few years after St. Martín's death to write his biography by members of the Dominican Province of St. John the Baptist (St. Martín's own province). In the preface, Medina states that he obtained his information through interviews with the Frailes of St. Martín's province as well as with people who had known him in Lima. Medina's biography was published in 1673. It was reprinted in various important sources, among them Melendez (1682, 201-346) and de Medina (n.d.). Medina's reprint in Melendez (1682) exists in only one copy which is found in the Rare Book room of the Library of Congress, Washington, D.C. The article in the Bollandist series, *Acta Sanctorum,* is a Latin translation of Medina's biography, which also contains an excellent list of the published lives of the saints. I have a contemporary reprint *San Martín de Porres: Biografía del Siglo XVII* (Mexico City, Editorial Jus, S.A., 1964, orig. ed. 1663). Ironically, Medina's biography was unknown and not referred to in any of the other biographies of St. Martín.

5. This was the same church in which that other great saint of Lima, Santa Rosa, was baptized a few years later.

6. The abrupt change of person in the quote is due to the fact that the account is a deposition given by an eyewitness and taken down by a notary. The notary often refers to the witness in the third person. The notary also recorded actual references by the eyewitness in the first or second person.

7. These laws were of great consequence, as Goodpasture (1989, 28) notes: "With regard to the priesthood, an early decision of the church came to have enormous consequences. The bishops ruled that no native Mexicans were to be prepared for ordination. The Indians could be interpreters, acolytes, and even teachers (*doctrineros*), but they were not allowed to be priests or to become members of the religious orders, male or female. Since the white population, both lay and clergy, was such a small minority among the native peoples and enjoyed such high privileges, and since the office of priest exerted considerable influence, the colonists felt more secure when native people were excluded from it." Although Goodpasture refers to Mexicans, these laws were widespread over Latin America.

8. Leonard Bernstein. *Mass.* A Theatre Piece for Singers, Players and Dancers. Conducted by the Composer. Text from the Liturgy of the Roman Mass. Celebrant sung by Alan Titus. Recorded at the Opening of the John F. Kennedy Center for the Performing Arts. Compact Disc. CBS Records M2K 44593. Actually the assertion that God is the "simplest of all" is a well-known principle in theology. One of Bonaventure's assertions, for example, is that although God is an absolute infinity, we finite human beings may know Him because God is also perfectly simple (Gilson 1965, 109).

9. The impact of the violent and unequal encounter of Europe and America has been discussed extensively. The literature is vast. Significant works include Baudet (1988), Chiapelli (1976), Elliott (1970), Gerbi (1973), Hanke (1959), Keen (1990). From the indigenous perspective, one can include León-Portilla (1963) and Brotherston (1979).

10. The classical understanding of difference was expressed either as a travelogue or diary, such as Herodotus' itinerary (an analysis of Herodotus' treatment of the "other" is found in Hartog (1988) or as a more substantial but second-hand encyclopedic form such as Pliny and Tacitus. The Christian codification of this "other" literature came with the Iberian bishop Isidore, who correlated the scriptural tradition to this classical literature (Dressel 1875: 207-68). Isidore's text may be found in Isidore of Seville (1911).

11. The actual passage reads as follows: "In my opinion, these animals are not tigers, nor are they panthers, or any other of the numerous known animals that have spotted skins, nor some new animal [of the 'old world'] that has a spotted skin and has not [yet] been described. The many animals that exist in the Indies that I describe here, or at least most of them, could not have been learned about from the ancients, since they exist in a land which had not been discovered until our own time. There is no mention made of these lands in Ptolemy's *Geography,* nor in any other work, nor were they known until Christopher Columbus showed them to us. . . But, returning to the subject already begun . . . this animal is called by the Indians ochi" (de Oviedo 1969, 11), quoted in Smith (1985, 3-48). Oviedo has been compared to the classical tradition of "difference" in López (1940), 1:46-61, 2:13-35. Moreover, one must not confuse this work, commonly called the *Sumario,* with his larger 1959 work.

12. The term *mestizo,* like the term *mulatto,* refers to the biological and cultural mixing due to a violent and unequal encounter of cultures. Mestizo is a common term in Latin America describing the offspring of Amerindian and Iberian parents. Virgilio Elizondo has expanded the term, however, to mean any biological and cultural mixing. An insightful and profound treatment of the meaning of the term *mestizo* may be found in Elizondo (1978b).

13. The term *mestizo* can become confusing. Mestizo, in a general sense, means someone who is of mixed race or mixed culture. Mestizo, in a particular sense, refers to someone who is an offspring of Iberian and indigenous race. The term *mulatto,* then, is a special instance of mestizo in the general sense but different from mestizo in the particular sense. I understand St. Martín to be specifically a mulatto but generally a mestizo.

2. FINDING THE "LITTLE STORY"

1. Arias (1977, 17) describes it as follows: "Even though the theological language is not yet clearly spelled out, it seems logical to speak of a popular religiosity to point to a way of religious expression in 'popular expressions' which are common to all religions, like dances, fiestas, dinners, etc. Currently, popular expressions do not coincide with official ones, whether by form or means. In those religious manifestations in which catholicism appears as an important element, even if it is mixed with religious elements from other cultures, one can speak of Popular Catholicism. Where catholic christianity is expressed with strength and dynamism to create traditions and expressions of faith, rooted in the existent cultures, one should speak of popular piety. To speak of popular religiosity we refer without distinction to all three, although we are conscious that there are great differences between all three."

2. As Luis Maldonado (1986, 3) puts it, "Medellín was concerned with popular religion for two reasons: first, that it was reacting against an elitist approach to pastoral practice, and secondly, that it was counteracting a pastoral practice characterized by a very European, particularly central-European, culture."

3. The concern of the left is described by Gilberto Gimenez (1978, 16): "The Church ought to be thought of as a 'heroic and committed minority,' with a high level of demands on its members. In these demands, it is included, in the first place, faith understood as option, as free and personal conviction. This conception is incompatible with an assumed 'church of the masses,' as would be the case with popular Catholicism, because the masses are fundamentally characterized by their passivity, inertia, and the law of least resistance. 'It lacks meaning,' says the Uruguayan theologian Juan Luis Segundo, 'to say that the Church, like every human group, has a range of adherents that goes from the most passive and liminal to the most active and responsible. Evangelical demands in the "umbral" are too selective.' "

4. The tension is described by Segundo Galilea (1976, 18): "An intensive pastoral focus has passed through inherent temptations. A tendency towards elitism, to concern itself with potential or actual militants. A certain spread of communities, groups or movements in themselves. A certain depreciation of what did not seem 'authentic christianity' (popular religiosity) and towards forms of 'multidarian pastoral work' or, extensive pastoral work. It seems that in the last years, at least in the convictions if not the acts themselves, an equilibrium is being sought in the name of the same mission of the elite christians and the nature of pastoral work, at times intensive and extensive. Christian communities discover, on one side, that their reason of being is mission among the masses, in the people alienated; on the other hand (specially the popular communities), they find that popular religiosity still goes on within them, even if purified."

5. Sociologist Robert Towler (1975, 147), contrasts popular religion with "official" religion: "If by official religion . . . we mean beliefs and practices which are

prescribed, regulated and socialized by specialized religious institutions, then common religion may be described as those beliefs and practices of an overtly religious nature which are not under domination of a prevailing religious institution."

6. Eugene Genovese (1976) used this understanding of hegemony to study slave religion in North America.

7. The same could be said of multiculturalism. Multiculturalism is a mixture of populism and pluralism. It offers the utopic ideal of a unified social body (a populist idea) out of different cultural groups (a pluralist goal). A problem with such a project is the fact that some powerful group must orchestrate such unity. Such orchestration takes place not by homogenizing cultural or social differences but by rendering them superficial or secondary to the goals of unity. My own sympathies lie with multiculturalism, but not in this form. I would prefer a movement that would celebrate many-culture rather than multi-culture. Many-culturalism would base a utopic ideal of unity of various cultural groups on the value of their very real differences. A many-cultural utopic ideal ultimately relies on the power of a "Big Story." The multicultural utopic ideal, I believe, ultimately relies on the power of some organizing social group. Lest I be misunderstood as throwing bricks at the many people involved in "multicultural" projects in the Church and in society, let me emphasize that while I am in sympathy with the utopic goals of "multiculturality," I believe that it is a concept flawed by its assumption that human differences are superficial. I respect and admire all those that take part in multicultural projects. Quite often, however, they are not involved in "multiculture" *per se* but in many-culture.

8. At issue here is the role of the individual with respect to his or her cultural heritage(s). Such a role can be expressed in one of two ways. Stated in its extreme form, one perspective sees culture as the cookie-cutter that stamps out individuals with culture. Another perspective sees culture as a toolkit or resource center through which a human being becomes an individual. The former does not explain the reality of the mestizo; the other does.

9. Actually, the first session for St. Martín's beatification process took place on June 15, 1658, and thirty witnesses were interrogated. The conveners of the process, however, realized that certain new regulations had not been followed and had to start over in 1660 (*Proceso*, 10).

10. I have a Spanish translation of the original Latin manuscript that is in the archives of the Archdiocese of Lima. A Spanish translation does not make my source entirely derivative. The only Latin in the Ordinary process concerned the acts of the process. The oaths, the questions put to the witnesses, the answers of the witnesses, etc., all were done in the vernacular; in the case of Lima, in Spanish. Thus, my Spanish "translation" still contains the actual testimony of the witnesses who participated in St. Martín's Ordinary process as recorded by the notary. Moreover, the Ordinary Process for St. Martín is extraordinarily detailed. The Lima Procurator must have been worried that the Apostolic process would be delayed.

3. READING THE "LITTLE STORY"

1. One could object that it is false to contrast language with signs in the context of culture. Language is, after all, a system of signs. Language is, of course, a system of signs, but it is also *one* instance of a system of signs derived from a culture. Other sign systems exist in culture that also provide the function of communication.

2. St. Augustine pioneered semiotics in order to make sense of obscure passages in Scripture (Colish 1968).

3. There are other definitions of sign, e.g., Saussure's dyadic sign consisting of only two elements, signifier and signified. Dyadic signs, however, lead to a closed system of communications, leaving culture as an inpermeable "bubble" of meaning. I find Peirce's definition the most adequate for the semiotics of culture, given the conditions of the violent and unequal encounter of cultures. A good source for definitions is Nöth (1990).

4. This is a reference to Clifford Geertz's proposal that culture be seen as "essentially semiotic. Believing, with Max Weber, that man is an animal suspended in webs of significance he himself has spun, I take culture to be those webs, and the analysis of it to be therefore not an experimental science in search of law but an interpretive one in search of meaning." His famous example for demonstrating this point was the difference between a twitch and a blink: "Consider he says, two boys rapidly contracting the eyelids of their right eyes. In one, this is an involuntary twitch; in the other, a conspiratorial signal to a friend. The two movements are identical . . . yet the difference . . . between a twitch and a wink is vast . . . Suppose," he continues, "there is a third boy, who 'to give malicious amusement to his cronies,' parodies the first boy's wink, as amateurish, clumsy, obvious, and so on. Here, too a socially established code exists . . . only now it is not conspiracy but ridicule that is in the air . . . [The] point is that between what Ryle calls the 'thin description' of what the rehearser . . . is doing . . . and the 'thick description' of what he is doing . . . lies the object of ethnography: a stratified hierarchy of meaningful structures in terms of which twitches, winks, fake-winks, parodies, rehearsals of parodies are produced, perceived, and interpreted" (Geertz 1973, 5-7).

5. Tillich's theology of culture is best understood in light of his love for the expressive and mediative power of the visual arts. It was a love developed in the mortal shadows falling on the trenches of German troops in World War I. John Dillenberger puts it as follows: "This interpretation of Tillich is confirmed by subsequent events. Tillich faced the ugliness and the terror of war for four years. He was subsequently decorated for his valor in trying circumstances. This war experience, which brought him to the edge of both physical and psychic collapse, was counterbalanced by his viewing works of art in whatever cheap reproductions he could find. He saw them as solace, order, and beauty, aspects of life threatened by the world of the trenches around him. Among the works that he knew from reproductions was Sandro Botticelli's *Madonna and Child with Singing Angels*. When he saw the actual painting while on leave in Berlin, the power of the original became a revelatory experience, an ecstatic encounter. While the painting belongs to the Renaissance world . . . the order, the beauty, and form of this painting was to the Tillich on leave from the battlefield an anchor in an uncertain world. Moreover, in Botticelli's work, especially in this painting, the sorrow of the world is suggested by the madonna's expression which is simultaneously joy-filled and melancholy. Beauty is not without its dark side" (Tillich 1987, xi).

6. The inner and outer perspective are based on the "emic"/ "etic" distinction cultural anthropologists make. Marvin Harris (1980, 32) describes the terms: "Emic operations have as their hallmark the elevation of the native informant to the status of ultimate judge of the adequacy of the observer's descriptions and analyses. The test of the adequacy of emic analyses is their ability to generate statements the native

accepts as real, meaningful, or appropriate . . . Etic operations have as their hallmark the elevation of observers to the status of ultimate judges of the categories and concepts used in descriptions and analyses. The test of the adequacy of etic accounts is simply their ability to generate scientifically productive theories about the causes of sociocultural differences and similarities." This is more than a distinction between objective and subjective points of view, since both the cultural insider's and cultural outsider's point of view may be presented subjectively or objectively. The distinction, as Harris points out, lies in the audience to whom the description is aimed. An etic description, for example, allows alien (to the observed culture) categories to be introduced. Such a description is appropriate for a specialist, i.e., professional or academic audience.

7. The inner-outer perspective parallels the emic-etic distinction. The inner perspective (corresponding to the emic description) is charaterized by narrative. It is concerned more with the telling of a story than with interpreting or translating it. It is a description "from the inside," the aim of which is to "reaffirm realities rather than dissect them." The test of an inner perspective is how well it reinforces the identity of the cultural "insider." The outer perspective, on the other hand, is less concerned with narrative than with analytic discourse. Narrative may be used in an outer perspective as a case study that sets the stage for a discourse of explanation. The test of an outer perspective is not the reaffirmation of identity for the cultural insider but the translation of that identity or reality into a sign system understood by the cultural outsider. Such a perspective inevitably uses categories that are alien to the observed culture (Schreiter 1985, 58-59).

8. The speaker-hearer pair of perspectives is based on a communications model. This pair of perspectives applies to both inner and outer perspectives, as it is central in any type of communication. A speaker-oriented perspective is "clear transmission of messages in the culture." The main concern here is distortion of the message originating with the speaker. As such, the hearer of the message "must be conformed to the message in both content and in its structure." Thus, the speaker controls the sign system. A hearer-oriented perspective, on the other hand, is akin to the perspective of an apologist. The principal issue concerns the ability "of the hearer to relate the message to his or her world." This means that the speaker will "vary the structure of the message (use variants in the sign system) in order to achieve maximum integration into the sign system of the hearer." In other words, the speaker does not feel compelled to transmit a message literally. The speaker feels free to change the style or the words, or even the order of the words themselves in order to transmit a traditional message (Schreiter 1985, 59).

9. Which perspective one chooses determines the nature of the analysis. The least adequate analysis occurs when perspectives are mixed. In a semiotics of culture, one's perspective needs to be identified and then followed consistently. The question of perspective impinges on our previous discussion on specialists. Specialist language, which serves only the specialist, occurs when perspectives are mixed. An anthropologist, for example, may use an outer perspective to collect data yet summarize the data using an inner perspective. Moreover, the same anthropologist may communicate his or her findings ostensibly as a hearer when, in fact, the findings are essentially presented from a speaker perspective. Thus, little communication takes place except, perhaps, among other specialists. There is nothing wrong with specialized language that serves to understand. Specialized language takes place when perspectives are

clearly identified. When perspective is used consistently, communication takes place and a story is told. Specialized language, in fact, is language proper to each perspective. Such language serves the goals of its intended perspective rather than the goals of the specialist.

10. The "little stories" of St. Martín de Porres will be told from both an outer and hearer perspective. I am a specialist, a theologian interested in communicating the value of the "little stories" of this popular tradition to members of my specialist community as well as to those who are not familiar with St. Martín de Porres. At the same time, I am an apologist for the "little stories" of popular religion and for St. Martín de Porres. My goals are the same as the goals of these two perspectives. One of my goals is to make possible communication between the more powerful world of the cultural outsider and the more vulnerable insider world of the "little story" hearers, many of whom happen to be Hispanic-Americans. My other goal is to protect and guide an important popular tradition of Hispanic-American Catholics beset by powerful centrifugal forces that are experienced as a minority culture lives a common ecclesial life within a more powerful dominant culture. Such goals, I believe, are proper to a specialist, a theologian of the church. The loss of the "little stories" of St. Martín de Porres would be more than a loss for Hispanic-American Catholics. It would be a loss for the entire Church. I believe that a "Big Story" of faith is being communicated through these little stories. It is my goal to demonstrate this thesis and communicate this "Big Story" to those who may not be familiar with it.

11. The definition of culture ranges widely, from Tylor's "complex whole" to Geertz's "webs of significance." There are, in fact, hundreds of definitions, although most can be roughly grouped under functionalist, materialist, or structuralist approaches. Two common principles appear to apply to all. Cultural phenomena deal with identity and with changes to that identity. Less than a definition but more than an arbitrary assumption, these two principles may be used to articulate an understanding of the basic concepts of the semiotics of culture. A somewhat dated but still useful survey of culture models is Kroeber and Kluckhohn (1952). A more recent survey is Harris (1968).

12. The semiosphere is actually based on classical communications theory that modeled the act of communication as consisting of an addresser who initiates a message. This message travels through a channel that links the addresser to an addressee who receives the message. Such a model, however, fails to account for cultural communication. As Lotman (1990, 123-24) explains it, "A schema consisting of addresser, addressee and the channel linking them together is not yet a working system [of communications]. For it to work it has to be 'immersed' in semiotic space. All participants in the communicative act must have some experience of communication, be familiar with semiosis. So, paradoxically, semiotic experience precedes the semiotic act. By analogy with the biosphere (Vernadsky's concept) we could talk of a semiosphere, which we shall define as the semiotic space necessary for the existence and functioning of languages, not the sum total of different languages; in a sense the semiosphere has a prior existence and is in constant interaction with languages . . . [Thus] . . . Outside the semiosphere, there can be neither communication nor language." There is, then, a circular nature to the semiosphere. On the one hand, like the biosphere, the individual units (of meaningful communication) constitute the semiosphere, yet it is the semiosphere which determines the nature of the individual units!

13. Lotman (1990, 125) puts it as follows: "So any one language turns out to be immersed in a semiotic space and it can only function by interaction with that space. The unit of semiosis, the smallest functioning mechanism, is not the separate language but the whole semiotic space of the culture in question. This is the space we term the semiosphere. The semiosphere is the result and the condition for the development of culture; we justify our term by analogy with the biosphere, as Vernadsky defined it, namely the totality and the organic whole of living matter and also the condition for the continuation of life."

14. The name of a semiosphere or semiotic domain, in fact, corresponds to a metaphor. Metaphor names semiospheres and semiotic domains. When a metaphor corresponds to an entire semiosphere, it is known as a root metaphor. The ability of metaphor to name a semiosphere or semiotic domain lies in its ability to link disparate signs together. Metaphor refers not to some individual sign or meaning but to a complex of linked signs. When this complex identifies a self-consistent set of signs capable of producing meaningful messages, that is, a sign system, the metaphor refers to a semiotic domain or semiosphere. Thus, one of the important techniques of the semiotics of culture identifies the recurrent metaphors of a cultural text. Such metaphors name the various semiotic domains of the cultural text which, in turn, determine the context through which the messages of a cultural text are to be understood. The prize in the semiotic analysis of a cultural text, however, is the root metaphor. The root metaphor contains within it all the semiotic domains pertaining to the cultural text. The root metaphor is the key to the context of the cultural text.

15. The ability to link signs together into a sign system gives metaphor another property. Metaphors not only have the ability to link signs together into a sign system but also have the ability to link or map entire sign systems. Thus to speak of wine as nectar is not to make a false identification but, rather, an apt analogy. In other words, metaphor serves to link two separate semiotic domains, creating new meanings. As such, metaphors have persuasive power in a culture. This power comes from the various accomplishments in each metaphorical linking or mapping. Lakoff (1989, 65) lists these accomplishments as follows: "Each metaphorical mapping consists of the following: [1] Slots in the source domain . . . get mapped onto slots in the target domain . . . In some cases the target domain slots exist independently of the metaphoric mapping . . . Other target domains are created by the mapping . . . [2] Relations in the source domain . . . get mapped onto relations in the target domain . . . [3] Properties in the source domain . . . get mapped onto properties in the target domain . . . [and, 4] Knowledge in the source domain gets mapped onto the source domain." Thus metaphoric mapping has the power to: (1) structure invisible or imagined universes; (2) increase the number of meaningful options in a semiotic domain; (3) borrow patterns of inference in one domain from another; (4) evaluate a semiotic domain from various points of view; and (5) experience one semiotic domain from the vantage point of another. In a semiotics of culture, then, metaphor serves a dual function. It establishes a semiotic domain that gives context to the signs, codes, and messages of a given culture and links separate domains together, providing additional meaning to the signs, codes, and messages in each domain.

16. Yuri Lotman, a Russian researcher in the semiotics of culture, describes a semiotic boundary as follows (1990, 131): "One of the primary mechanisms of semiotic individuation is the boundary, and the boundary can be defined as the outer limit of a first-person form. This space is 'ours,' 'my own', it is 'cultured,' 'safe,'

'harmoniously organized,' and so on. By contrast, 'their space' is 'other,' 'hostile,' 'dangerous,' 'chaotic.' Every culture begins by dividing the world into 'its own' internal space and 'their' external space. How this binary division is interpreted depends on the typology of the culture. But the actual division is one of the human cultural universals. The boundary may separate the living from the dead, settled people from nomadic ones, the town from the plains; it may be a state frontier, or a social, national, confessional, or any other kind of frontier." The semiotic boundary describes, then, what Lotman calls an Internal (I) and an External (E) space. The relationship between (I) and (E) is a series of antitheses which make up the identity of the culture. Since (I) is internal to a boundary, it suggests a more fundamental antithesis. Since (I) is basically a "closed" world, only a finite range of possibilities pertain to it. (E), on the other hand, is an "open" world exposed to an infinite number of possibilities. This natural difference leads to the fundamental antithesis: organized vs. disorganized or order versus chaos. Indeed, by looking at ordering principles within a culture, one can be led to the fundamental semiotic boundary of the culture. Conversely, having identified a semiotic boundary, one can demonstrate the ordering principle of a culture.

17. Signs, as bearers of messages in a culture, serve to create messages of identity or difference which, in turn, function as boundary markers. An example of signs of identity or solidarity are the familiar pronouns (e.g., Spanish *tu,* German *du*). The use of the Spanish *tu,* for instance, may signify solidarity. The use of the Spanish *vos,* on the other hand, may signify difference. Signs of difference and solidarity, however, rely on a more fundamental distinction: asymmetry versus symmetry. Asymmetry serves to exclude or contradict other signs. Asymmetry gives signs the capacity to carry messages of change. Symmetry, on the other hand, serves to connect or duplicate signs. Symmetry gives signs the capacity to clarify messages of identity. Asymmetry and symmetry, however, may also include relationships of reciprocity and nonreciprocity. As such, asymmetry and symmetry also give signs the capacity to carry messages about power relationships. *Vos,* for example, may represent either a family member such as one's grandmother or a feared supervisor. The relationship with the grandmother is one of reciprocity based on symmetrical family relationships, but the relationship with the feared supervisor is one of nonreciprocity based on the asymmetrical relationship of unequal power. Thus the sign *vos* may signify more than simple difference but also a power difference. A careful analysis of the cultural text is needed to ascertain these important distinctions (Hodge and Kress 1988, 40-44).

18. St. Martín fighting with demons is an example of another fundamental antithesis in a large number of cultural "texts," what Lotman calls (A) or the visible world, the earthly world, "this" world and (Z) the invisible world, the unearthly, "that" world. The superimposition of the (A)-(Z) antithesis on the (I)-(E) antithesis often occurs. One variant of the superimposition is the absorption of the (I)-(E) boundary into the "inner" space of the (A)-(Z) antithesis. In other words, the boundary between (I) and (E) becomes dissolved inside the new inner world which is (A) or "this" world. The "outer" world is now (Z) and it is the inhabitant of the invisible. Thus, the Hispanic-American frustrating his supervisor becomes not only one of "them" but also "invisible," "invisible" to promotion, to merit raises, and, so forth.

A further replication, however, occurs of the antithesis (I)-(E) into (Z). The invisible world is divided into zones of "good" and "bad" corresponding to the "we"/"they" dichotomy of the first antithesis. Thus demons inhabit the bad (Z) while angels inhabit the good (Z) while both us (I) and them (E) live in this world (A). The significance for a religious cultural text is that discourse over events of that world may be used to say something about this world. Moreover, the discourse over relationships between this world and that world may be used to say something about our world and their world. When St. Martín de Porres fights a demon, something else is also being said about this world (Lotman 1975, 110-11).

19. Binary oppositions make possible the transformation of meaning in a culture. The transformation of meaning allows a culture to negotiate change successfully by changing the relation between signs and their messages or changing the codes themselves. Such transformations may either be incorporative through a process which brings new signs, codes, and messages into the semiotic system, or conflictual through a process in which one set of signs, codes, and messages is eliminated and replaced by another. An example of an incorporative process of semiotic transformation is religious syncretism. The Virgin of Guadalupe, for example, appeared in the same place where Tonantzin, the Aztec goddess, was worshiped. Such a process, however, is only possible when the culture in change has sufficient resources for strength of identity to take on such new realities. As long as the fundamental sign systems of a culture are strong enough to remain in control such an incorporative process can take place.

An example of a conflictual process of semiotic transformation is the colonialization process, where the more powerful colonial government imposes a sign system whose purpose is to replace the sign system of the colonized. Another example involves inner conflict between sign systems in which one group finds the prevailing sign system inadequate or irrelevant and supplants it with a new set of signs, codes, and messages. The French and Russian revolutions may be cited as examples. Another process, however, is possible. A hegemonic process of accommodation and resistance, for example, relies on giving signs a bivalency that means one thing to the powerful group and another to the less powerful. Such double meanings can come together in very creative communicative webs which, in effect, transform the more powerful system of signs into a new system of signs that allows the weaker group to navigate the changes imposed by the powerful (See Schreiter 1985, 70-71).

4. THE VIOLENT AND UNEQUAL ENCOUNTER OF CULTURES

1. The native name for the river, Rimac, which means murmur was corrupted to Lima by the Spanish propensity to soften r's. *Rimac* is a Quechua word meaning speaker. *Enciclopedia Universal Ilustrada Europeo-Americana* s.v. "Lima" (Madrid: Espasa-Calpe, S.A., 1967). According to Prescott, the Incas named the river "speaker" because of a temple in the valley in which oracles were heard (n.d., 1007). There is a small subaltern note to make here: Lima's indigenous "speaker" was not silenced by the Conquistadores.

2. The effect of plague on human populations is well treated in McNeill (1976).

3. Borah and Cook estimate an initial population of 25.3 million Central Mexican indigenous on the eve of the conquest in 1519, compared to 1 million by 1605. Assuming the same rate of decline, Peru's indigenous population would have fallen from a 1520 estimate of 14.4 million to a 1570 estimate of 1.3 million (Cook 1981, 53).

4. Jose de Acosta described the richness of the mine. "It appears from the royal

accounts of the House of Trade of Potosí, and it is affirmed by venerable and trustworthy men, that during the time of the government of the licentiate Polo, which was many years after the discovery of the hill, silver was registered every Saturday to the value of 150 to 200,000 pesos, of which the King's fifth (quintos) came to 30 to 40,000 pesos, making a yearly total of about 150,000 pesos. According to this calculation, the value of the daily output of the mine was 30,000 pesos of which the King's share amounted to 6,000 pesos" (Keen 1986, 82).

5. Jack Weatherford put it as follows: "At the time of the discovery of America, Europe had only about $200 million worth of gold and silver, approximately $2 per person. By 1600 the supply of precious metals had increased approximately eightfold. The Mexican mint alone coined $2 billion worth of silver pieces of eight" (Weatherford 1988, 10-11). Adam Smith documented the effect of this increase in wealth in his classic study of the market system (1937, 200-5). The classic study on the effect of the importation of precious metals from America on the European economy is Hamilton (1934).

6. The literature on the Atlantic slave trade and Latin America is growing. Important books include Bowser (1974), Klein (1967, 1986), Patterson (1982), and Rout (1976).

7. The demographic collapse took place most quickly in the Antilles. As early as 1526, a letter from the bishop of the diocese of San Juan (the early name for Puerto Rico) sent this letter to Charles V: "Don Alonso Manzo, Bishop of San Juan and Inquisitor of the Indies; because many indians given to me by your Majesty for my sustenance have died of sickness, I ask license for your servant to buy 20 black slaves" (Soler 1953, 44).

8. A more complete discussion can be found in Mrner (1967).

9. The Dominicans had arrived at Lima with Pizarro and thus were the first Order to arrive in Peru. When Pizarro founded Lima, he assigned a plot of land for the construction of their convent, which came to be called "Nuestra Señora del Rosario." In 1539, Pope Paul III created the Dominican province of St. John the Baptist of Peru and made Nuestra Señora del Rosario convent the site of "Estudio General" by royal decree from Charles V with all the privileges of the University of Salamanca (Crespo 1964, 66).

10. The text of these bulls can be found in Zavala (1984) and Parry and Keith (1984).

11. The decree read, "In order to accomplish the salvation of the souls of said Indians employed by those people who are there, it is necessary that the Indians be apportioned to different communities so that they may live together [so that] they stop doing the things that until now they used to do, that they may stop bathing, painting themselves, and purging themselves as often as they do now" (Pacheco and de Mendoza 1864-84, 9-13).

12. The introduction of Aristotle in medieval anthropology comes from the twelfth century Renaissance of Aristotelian philosophy brought about by the Reconquista and subsequent contact with the Moors who had access to Aristotle's writings. This Scholastic appropriation of Aristotle's anthropology was applied to consequent contact of Europe with the Tartars. The details can be found in Jones (1971), 376-407.

13. The first protest emerging against the Encomienda came from the Dominican Fray Antonio de Montesinos, who in his Advent Sunday sermon of 1511 warned the colonists that their participation in the Encomienda structure was a mortal sin and

they were in grave danger of losing their souls. In March 1512, Montesino's provincial superior, Alonso de Loysa, sharply reprimanded Montesino and warned him not to dwell on theological matters which "are no concern of monks" (Padgen 1986, 30-31).

14. The question has often been asked as to the course of history if Columbus, like Cortez, had first landed in Mexico rather than the Antilles.

15. I have a copy of the critical edition published in 1892 (Sepúlveda, 260-381).

16. On the eve of the debate with Las Casas, Sepúlveda had just completed and published (Paris 1548) his Latin translation of the *Politics* of Aristotle (Green 1940, 340).

17. There is much indirect evidence that this perspective was the majority perspective as Vitoria, even before Sepúlveda, gave arguments to various unknown proponents of this perspective (Hanke 1959, 31).

18. The argument is found in the forty-fourth distinctio of Mair's commentary on the second of Peter Lombard's *Sentences.* "These people [the Amerindians] live like beasts on either side of the equator; and beneath the poles there are wild men as Ptolemy says in his Tetrabiblos. And this has now been demonstrated by experience, wherefore the first person to conquer them, justly rules over them because they are by nature slaves. As the Philosopher [Aristotle] says in the third and fourth chapters of the first book of the *Politics,* it is clear that some men are by nature slaves, others by nature free; and in some men it is determined that there is such a thing [i.e., a disposition to slavery] and that they should benefit from it. And it is just that one man should be a slave and another free, and it is fitting that one man should rule and another obey, for the quality of leadership is also inherent in the natural master. On this account the Philosopher says in the first chapter of the afore mentioned book that this is the reason why the Greeks should be masters over the barbarians because, by nature, the barbarians and slaves are the same" (Padgen 1986, 39).

19. As Sepúlveda puts it: "Compare, then, with the prudence, ingenuity, generous spirit, temperance, humanity and religion of these men those 'diminished-men' in which few aspects of humanity are found" (1892, 309).

20. The presentation on the Salamanca School follows closely Padgen's own (1986, 57-108), so I will not reference the presentation unless deviating from Padgen. Other presentations on the Salamanca School can be found in Fernández-Santamaria (1977), Copleston (1968), and Carro (1945).

21. The classical phrase used to describe Natural Law is "in cordibus hominum" or "in the hearts of men" and is found in Augustine (1961), bk.2, ch. 4. This phrase was synonymous with the term "natural law" and was believed to be put "in the hearts of men" at Creation.

22. Vitoria wrote his friend, P. Miguel de Arcos, that "his blood had turned to ice" when he heard about the execution of the Inca Atahualpa (Arciniegas 1980).

23. As Padgen puts it (1986, 66): "The Spaniard's rights to conquer and settle Indian territories, which had always seemed to be a legal question, was, in fact, Vitoria was now maintaining, a theological one, for only the theologians were equipped to discuss the divine law. Thus since theology is concerned with essentials not accidents and since its prime business is the analysis and explanation of things about whose reality there can be no doubt (*res certa*), it was perfectly legitimate for the theologian to reopen the Indian question."

24. De Vitoria's actual wording was: "That these barbarians, although, as we have said, are not altogether incapable are, however, not too far removed from those that

are mentally backwards that it seems that they are not fit to constitute and administer a legitimate republic within human and political limits" (1967, 3.17).

25. This list of "arts" is the list given by Aristotle for distinguishing a barbarian from a civilized society. Vitoria, then, in reference to the perceived barbarism of the "advanced" Indian, "approached the subject from the other end, listing this time not what the Indians had in common with civilized men, but what they did not have" (Padgen 1981, 71-112).

26. Again, in Vitoria's own words, "This can be shown, because in reality they are not idiots but have, in their manner, the use of reason. It is evident that they have a certain order in their things: that they have duly governed cities, well arranged marriages, magistrates, lords, laws, professors, industries, commerce which all requires the use of reason. Besides they have a form of religion and do not err in those things which are evident to others which is a sign of the use of reason (usus rationis). God and nature has not abandoned them in what is indispensable for the species, and what is principal for man is reason and potentiality which does not become actuality is useless" (1967, 1.15.5-20).

27. Pierre La Primaudaye, for example, uses Lycurgus' dogs to examine the effect of custom on the diversity of newly "found" peoples in *Academie Françoise, en laquelle il est traitté de l'institution des moeurs e de ce qui concerne le bien et hereusment vivre,* 3rd ed. (Paris: University of Paris, 1580). The connection to the semiotic analysis in which dogs play a major sign should not be lost.

28. Padgen's assessment is as follows: "*De indis* effectively destroyed the credibility of the theory of natural slavery as a means to explain the deviant behavior of the Indian. After Vitoria's analysis it was clear to all his followers that as a model, as a paradigm, it had failed dismally to satisfy the evidence it was intended to explain. Henceforth the Indian would cease to be any form of 'natural man'—however that ambiguous phrase might be interpreted. He was now, whatever his shortcomings, like all other men, a being whose actions could only be adequately explained in terms of his culture" (1986, 104-5).

29. Nonetheless, these "new" worlds could be brought under the ancient categories of "Ethiopia" and "Asia" even as they posed real challenges of classification using classical sources of authority.

30. As Gerbi (1973, 581) puts it, "When the Renaissance dawned and nature rose to the supreme rank, to paradigm of rationality and perfection, honored and studied for herself, and finally even hypostatized as God, the impotence or negligence of nature should have disappeared. But the dualism, however much refuted and suppressed, continually reemerges from the bosom of that physical unity postulated and proclaimed as absolute. Except that instead of generically investing all creation it insisted on its critical principle in specific reference to this or that section of the universe. Instead of being evenly diluted, so to speak, over the infinite scale of beings, from God all the way down to the last grain of sand, it concentrated on the recent impressive acquisitions of geography and physics, and expressed itself in characteristic form in the duality of Old and New World, the one mature and the other immature, or the one perfect and the other imperfect, one the creation of the fully realized power of nature, the other an unhappy abortion of its impotence, or later, with the positions reversed."

31. The Jesuit Peter Claver saw the just title used for the Amerindian also used to enslave the African. "It is well known to all that in purchasing and transporting

Negroes from their own country to the Indies and here (Spain) endless trickery and numberless acts of robbery and violence are committed . . . Under the pretext of a just war, many and mostly unjust wars are waged, for as they (the Negroes) are uncivilized, they are not moved by reason but by passion; they do not examine or consider their rights" (Valtierra 1960, 94-95).

32. Keen offers this telling quote (1986, 120): "Turning now to the persons called mestizos and mulattoes, of whom there are great numbers in the Indies, first let me say that the name mestizo was assigned to the former because they represent a mixture of blood and nationality. . . . As for the mulattoes, although for the same reason they belong in the class of mestizos, yet as the offspring of Negro women and white men or the reverse, which is the most strange and repulsive mixture of all, they bear this specific name which compares them to the species of the mule." This attitude is seen in the "little stories" which involve mules.

33. The attitudes toward freedmen and women is depicted here by Bowser (1974, 302). "The Spanish community of Peru regarded the free person of African descent with marked ambivalence. Color prejudice and presumed illegitimacy doomed most free Afro-Peruvians to the ranks of the disadvantaged, and it was easy for Spaniards to characterize them in the mass as 'a band of troublemakers, abetting runaway slaves, covering up thefts, fomenting unrest.' " Yet day-to-day experience was studded with examples indicating that free coloreds were "an industrious and useful class of people who seized every opportunity given them, and did much to build up the country for themselves and the Spaniards." In short, the free person of color presented a "double image to the Spanish, an image that was reflected in Peruvian law and reality. In law, the free person of color was closely identified with the slave, and most restrictions and reminders of inferior status were applied to both, though the free man was sometimes penalized less heavily for violations. In his free status, the person of color also assumed many of the burdens expected of the Indian and the Spaniard: like the Indian, he was obliged to pay tribute and was not supposed to be idle; like the Spaniard, he was expected to defend the state by serving in the militia and was subject to the supervision of the Holy Office. In addition, free coloreds of mixed blood and illegitimate birth had to deal with a peculiar prejudice faced by neither white nor brown nor black."

34. A spirited defense in favor of the Indians receiving the Eucharist is found in Agurto (1573).

5. DOG STORIES AND A LADDER

1. This approach, however, is not necessarily a history of religions. The semiotics of culture differs from a history of religions that takes signs out of their native semiosphere to compare them with other signs from other semiospheres. While semiotics is also interested in the signs constructing the religious texts of a culture, it would be an act of semiotic violence to disengage them somehow from their native semiosphere. Thus, the sign "moon" may be shown to be comparable to similar signs in other cultures in a history of religions. This is what Mircea Eliade does in his well-known *Patterns in Comparative Religion* (1963). A semiotics of culture would consider the sign "moon" as having proper meaning only in the various interrelationships with other signs present in its native semiosphere. This does not mean that a history of religions is an invalid science but that the goals are different. Nonetheless,

signs from a history of religions approach may be useful in establishing the primordiality of certain signs. Such signs would be important signifiers in any semiosphere.

2. The search for recurrent metaphors (or signs) took place through the use of a computer database based on the "little stories" of the *Proceso*. Categorized by theme and keywords, a search of the story database uncovered clusters of stories and patterns that form part of the basis for the following.

3. I am not referring here to Lovejoy's (1960) concept of the "Great Chain of Being" but to a theological principle active in Ibero-European theology of the sixteenth and seventeenth centuries.

4. Boethius' definition was *naturae rationalis individua substantia* as recorded in *Contra Eutychen* and translated by Gilson (1940, 201). *See* Copleston (1968, 103).

5. One can see the use of the ladder to represent the hierarchy of being in a diagram printed by Raymond Lull in 1512 in his *Liber de ascensu et descensu intellectus* and reprinted in Hodgen (1964), 401.

6. THE ILL AND THE WOUNDED

1. By this, I am referring to the "sweet" smells emanating from the corpses of martyrs and saints as reported by their witnesses. This phenomenon has been given the most attention by Thurston (1952, 222-32). The earliest record of such a phenomenon is in the *Acts of Martyrs* in a "little story" concerning the martyrdom in A.D. 155 of St. Polycarp. During Polycarp's conflagration, the *Acts* reports that "a smell like incense or myrrh or some other precious ointment dispelled all other bad odors due to the fire" (Bueno 1968, 275).

2. The "discipline" or *las disciplinas* consisted of leather or chain thongs with which a penitent would whip himself ritually in order to "mortify" his body toward a spiritual goal. St. Dominic is well known to have taken three such disciplines a day.

3. This hierarchy is not necessarily along class lines. Race and cultural background play a major role. The hierarchy is described in detail in Burkholder and Johnson (1990).

8. THE ANTHROPOLOGY OF CREATURELINESS

1. I am aware of the philosophical problems that the existence of a one-of-a-kind "being" creates. To discuss them in this work, however, would not be appropriate. Let it suffice to say that the very nature of the human refers to an ontology and a relationship. Humans are one-of-a-kind as far as God is concerned. The emphasis here is on the relationship. Humans, however, are also creatures among others. The emphasis here is on the ontology. For this reason, I avoid the language of "being" when referring to the human as much as possible.

2. The cosmos as a fecund variety of creatures is one of the most ancient human understandings of Nature. *See* Glacken (1967).

3. This assertion is similar to Aquinas' view of the human being as *tabula rasa,* an empty tablet on which the experiences of life would write one's character. Yet it is an assertion I make with qualifications. Finding an "identity" is not the same as having an identity written on a *tabula rasa.*

4. A good introduction to the imagination can be found in Kearney (1988). The following is based on this work. Other important works on the imagination include

Brann (1991), Tracy (1981), and Warnock (1978). Tracy's work is a well-known work on the relation between theology and the imagination.

5. I am referring, of course, to the origins of human existence as told by the "little story" of Adam and Eve. To participate in the imagination of the Creator is to "remember" the original meaning of human existence, an existence Adam and Eve pointed to in the "little stories" of the Church's traditional "Big Story."

6. The perceptive reader who detects here a trace of Bonaventure's theology of Creation along with his Platonic principle of exemplarism is correct. A qualification has to be mentioned, however. The guiding vision for this admittedly sketchy theology of Creation is similar to a Bonaventuran type of cosmic exemplarism whose "examples" or "forms" originate in the mind of God, except that it has been thoroughly imbued with the notions emerging from Sullivan's work as well as Schreiter's semiotics of culture. My cosmic "exemplarism" is not based so much on "forms" originating in the mind of God as they are signs pointing to what Sullivan calls the origins of "differences," the origins where the fecundity of Creation begins. As such, the origin of "differences" is, for me, the imagination of the Creator and the place where all signs originate. Not much more, unfortunately, can be said in the brevity of an endnote.

7. Healing in the cosmic sense, at least the way I mean it, takes up both the Augustinian notion of grace as restoration or healing as well as Aquinas' sense of grace as "perfecting" or "completing" nature.

Bibliography

Acuña, Rodolfo. 1981. *Occupied America: A History of Chicanos.* 2d ed. New York: Harper & Row Publishers.

Adorno, Rolena. 1986. *Guaman Poma: Writing and Resistance in Colonial Peru.* Institute of Latin American Studies, vol. 68. Austin: University of Texas Press.

Agurto, Pedro, O.S.A. 1573. *Tractado de que se Deven Administrar los Sacramentos de la Sancta Eucharistia y Extrema Unción a los Indios de esta Nueva España.* Mexico.

Alphonsus, Mary. 1968. *St. Rose of Lima: Patroness of the Americas.* Rockford, IL: Tan Books and Publishers.

Alvarez, Manuel Diaz. 1987. *Léxico del Mestizaje en Hispanoamerica.* Madrid: Ediciones Cultura Hispanica.

Anonymous. 1958. *Enciclopedia Universal Ilustrada Europeo-Americana.* Madrid: Espasa-Calpe, S.A. s.v. "Lima."

Aquinas, St. Thomas. 1964. *Summa Theologiae.* Blackfriars edition with Latin Text and English Translation, Introduction, Notes, Appendices, and Glossaries. 60 vols. New York: McGraw-Hill.

_____. 1975. *Summa Contra Gentiles.* Trans. Charles O'Neil. 5 vols. Notre Dame, IN: University of Notre Dame Press.

Archer, John. 1673. *Compendious Herbal.* London.

Arciniegas, Gérman. 1980. *América en Europa.* Bogotá: Plaza & Janes, S.A. Orig. ed. 1975.

Arias, Maximino. 1977. *Religiosidad Popular en América Latina.* In *Iglesia y Religiosidad Popular en América Latina: Ponencias y Documento.* Bogotá: Secretariado General del CELAM, 17-44.

Aristotle. 1984. *The Complete Works of Aristotle*. Ed. Jonathan Barnes. Vol. 1. *Nicomachean Ethics*. Princeton, NJ: Princeton University Press.

Augustine, Aurelius. 1954. *Quaestiones in Heptateuchum*. In *Corpus Christianorum*. Series Latina. Turnhout: Brepols.

_____. 1961. *Confessions*. Trans. R. S. Pine-Coffin. Hammondsworth: Penguin Classics.

_____. 1972. *The City of God*. Trans. Henry Bettenson. With an introduction by David Knowles. Harmondsworth, Middlesex, England: Penguin.

Baudet, Henri. 1988. *Paradise on Earth: Some Thoughts on European Images of Non-European Man*. Middletown, CT.: Wesleyan University Press.

Bellah, Robert. 1964. "Religious Evolution." *American Sociological Review* 29.

Benedict, Ruth. 1961. *Patterns of Culture*. Boston: Houghton Mifflin Co.

Blaher, Damian Joseph, O.F.M. 1949. *The Ordinary Processes in Causes of Beatification and Canonization: A Historical Synopsis and Commentary*. Ph. D. Diss. The Catholic University of America.

Boggs, Carl. 1976. *Gramsci's Marxism*. London: Pluto Press, Ltd.

Bonino, Jose Miguez. 1977. *Doing Theology in a Revolutionary Situation*. Philadelphia: Fortress Press.

Borges, Jorge Luis. 1964. "The Garden of Forking Paths." In *Labyrinths: Selected Stories and Other Writings*. Trans. Donald A. Yates and James E. Irby. With a preface by André Maurois. New York: New Directions Publishing Company, 19-58.

Bowser, Frederick P. 1972. *Colonial Spanish America*. In *Neither Slave nor Free: The Freedmen of African Descent in the Slave Societies of the New World*. Ed. David W. Cohen and Jack P. Greene. Baltimore, MD: The Johns Hopkins University Press, 19-58.

_____. 1974. *The African Slave in Colonial Peru 1524-1650*. Stanford, CA: Stanford University Press.

Brann, Eva. 1991. *The World of the Imagination*. Lanham, MD: Rowman & Littlefield Publishers, Inc.

Brotherston, Gordon. 1979. *Image of the New World: The American Continent Portrayed in Native Texts*. Trans. Ed Dorn. London: Thames & Hudson, Ltd.

Brown, Peter. 1981. *The Cult of the Saints: Its Rise and Function in Latin Christianity.* Chicago: University of Chicago Press.

Bueno, Daniel Ruiz, ed. 1968. *Actas de los Martires.* 2nd ed. Biblioteca de Autores Cristianos. Madrid: La Editorial Catolica, S.A.

Burke, Peter. 1984. "How to Be a Counter-reformation Saint." In *Religion and Society in Early Modern Europe 1500-1800.* Ed. Kaspar von Greyerz. London: George Allen & Unwin, Ltd.

Burkholder, Mark A., and Lyman L. Johnson. 1990. *Colonial Latin America.* Oxford: Oxford University Press.

Burridge, Kenneth. 1991. *In the Way.* Vancouver: University of British Columbia Press.

Busschof, Herman. 1676. *Two Treatises, the One Medical of the Gout.* By W.C. and sold by Moses Pitt.

Cajetan, Cardinal (Tommaso de Vio). 1888-1906. *Sancti Thomae Aquinatis Doctoris Angelica Opera Omnia Cum Commentaris Thomae de Vio Caetani.* 12 vols. Commentary on St. Thomas Aquinas' *Summa Theologica.* Rome: N.p.

Calame-Griaule, Geneviève. 1986. "Diseases and Cures." Trans. Brunhilde Biebuyck. In *The Encyclopedia of Religion.* Ed. Mircea Eliade. New York: Macmillan, 226-34.

Candelaria, Michael R. 1990. *Popular Religion and Liberation: The Dilemma of Liberation Theology.* Albany, NY: State University of New York Press.

Canedo, Lino Gómez. 1977. *Evangelización y Conquista: Experiencia Franciscana en Hispanoamérica.* Mexico City: Editorial Porrúa.

Canvet, Mariette. 1936- . "Sens Spirituel." In Marcel Viller S.J., ed. *Dictionnaire de Spiritualité.* Paris: Beauchesne, 1936- , 165-78.

Carro, V. 1945. *La Teología y los Teólogo-Juristas Españoles Ante la Conquista de Indias.* Seville: N.p.

Carroll, Patrick James. 1991. *Blacks in Colonial Veracruz: Race, Ethnicity, and Regional Development.* Austin, TX: University of Texas Press.

Cavallini, Giuliana. 1963. *Saint Martin de Porres: Apostle of Charity.* Rockford, IL: Tan Books and Publishers.

Chenu, M. D. 1968. *Nature, Man and Society in the Twelfth Century: Essays on New Theological Perspectives in the Latin West.* Translation of *La théologie au douz-*

ième siècle. Orig. ed. 1957. With a preface by Etienne Gilson. Trans. Jerome Taylor and Lester K. Little. Chicago: University of Chicago Press.

Chiapelli, Fred, ed. 1976. *First Images of America: The Impact of the New on the Old.* 2 vols. Berkeley, CA: University of California Press.

Clissold, Stephen. 1972. *The Saints of South America.* London: Charles Knight & Co., Limited.

Cobo, Bernabe. 1979. *History of the Inca Empire: An Account of the Indians' Customs and Their Origin Together with a Treatise on Inca Legends, History, and Social Institutions.* Trans. Roland Hamilton. With a foreword by John Rowe. Austin, TX: University of Texas Press. Orig. ed. 1653.

————. 1990. *Inca Religion and Customs.* Austin, TX: University of Texas Press.

Colish, Marcia L. 1968. *The Mirror of Language: A Study in the Medieval Theory of Knowledge.* Rev. ed. Lincoln, NE, and London: University of Nebraska Press.

Cook, David Noble. 1981. *Demographic Collapse: Indian Peru, 1520-1620.* Cambridge: Cambridge University Press.

Copleston, Frederick. 1968. *A History of Philosophy.* Vol. 3. *Ockham to Suárez.* The Bellamine Series. London: Burns and Oates.

Cortés, Hernan. 1986. *Letters from Mexico.* Ed. and trans. Anthony Padgen. 2d ed. New Haven, CN: Yale University Press.

Coseriu, Eugenio. 1970. *Die Geschichte der Sprachphilosophie von der Antike bis zur Gegenwart.* Tübingen: TBL.

Crespo, Pedro Rodriguez. 1964. *Biblioteca Hombres del Peru.* Vol. 5. *San Martín de Porres.* Lima: Antonio Miro Quesada.

Cret, Paul. 1907. "Animals in Christian Art." In *The Catholic Encyclopedia.* Ed. Charles G. Herbermann. Vol. 1. New York: Robert Appleton Company, 515-7.

Crosby, Alfred W., Jr. 1972. *The Columbian Exchange: Biological and Cultural Consequences of 1492.* Westport, CT.: Greenwood Press.

Davies, Brian. 1992. *The Thought of Thomas Aquinas.* New York: Oxford University Press.

de Acosta, Jose. 1940. *Historia Natural y Moral de Las Indias.* Critical Edition. Gorman O, E. Mexico City: N.p. Orig. ed. 1590-1608.

de Chardin, Pierre Teilhard. 1960. *The Divine Milieu.* Translation of *Le Milieu Divin.* Orig. ed. 1957. New York: Harper and Row, Harper Torchbooks/ Library.

_____. 1965. *The Phenomenon of Man*. With an introduction by Sir Julian Huxley. 2d ed. New York: Harper and Row, Harper Torchbooks/ Cathedral Library.

de la Primaudaye, Pierre. 1580. *Academie Françoise, en Laquelle Il Est Traitté de L'institution Des Moeurs e de Ce Qui Concerne le Bien et Heruesment Vivre*. 3d ed. Paris: University of Paris.

de la Vega, Garcilaso, El Inca. 1966. *Royal Commentaries of the Incas and General History of Peru*. Trans. Harold Livermore. With a foreword by Arnold Toynbee. Vol. 1, Part 1. Austin, TX: University of Texas Press.

de las Casas, Bartolomé. 1988. *Obras Completas*. Ed. Angel Losada. Vol. 9. *Apologiae Adversus Genesium Sepulvedam*. Madrid: Alianza Editorial. Orig. ed. 1550.

de Medina, Bernardo, O.P. N.d. "De Beato Martino de Porras Tertiario Professo O.S. Dominici." In *Acta Sanctorum*. Vol. 3. Brussels: Apud Socio Bollandiana.

_____. 1964. *San Martin de Porres: Biografía del Siglo XVII*. Mexico City: Editorial Jus, S.A. Orig. ed. 1663.

de Mercado, Tomás. 1587. *Suma de Tratos y Contratos*. Seville.

de Oviedo, Fernandez. 1959. *Historia General y Natural de Las Indias y Tierra-Firme del Mar Oceano*. Reprint of 1851-55 Edition of José Amador de los Riós (Madrid). Madrid: Biblioteca de Autores Españoles. Orig. ed. 1535.

_____. 1969. *De la Natural Hystoria de Las Indias*. Facsimile Edition. Chapel Hill, NC: University of North Carolina Press. Orig. ed. 1526.

de Pacchioni, Neri Romero. N.d. *La Fascinante Vida del Santo Martín de Porres*. Lima: Centro de Proyección Cristiana.

de Sandoval, Alonso. 1627. *Naturaleza, Policía Sagrada y Profana, Costumbres, Ritos y Supersticiones de los Etíopes (Negros)*. Seville.

de Vitoria, Francisco. 1967. *Relectio de Indis*. Critical Edition. In *Corpus Hispanorum de Pace*. Ed. & trans. L. Pereña and J. M. Prendes. Madrid: Consejo Superior de Investigaciones Científicas. Orig. ed. 1539.

_____. *Political Writings*. 1991. Ed. Anthony Padgen and Jeremy Lawrance. Cambridge Texts in the History of Political Thought. Cambridge: Cambridge University Press.

Deleuze, Gilles. 1981. *Différence et Répétition*. Paris: Presses Universitaires de France.

Dobyns, Henry F. 1963. "An Outline of Andean Epidemic History to 1720." *Bulletin of the History of Medicine* 37: 493-515.

Dressel, E. 1875. "De Isidori Originum Fontibus." *Rivista di Filologia e di Instruzione Classica* 3: 207-68.

Dussel, Enrique. 1974. *Historia de la Iglesia en América Latina.* Barcelona: Editorial Nova Terra.

_____, ed. 1983. *Historia General de la Iglesia en América Latina.* CEHILA. Vol. 1. *Introducción General a la Historia de la Iglesia en América Latina.* Salamanca: Ediciones Sígueme.

_____, ed. 1987. *Historia General de la Iglesia en América Latina.* CEHILA. Vol. 8. *Peru, Bolivia, y Ecuador.* Salamanca: Ediciones Siguéme.

Eames, Wilberforce. 1922. "Description of a Wood Engraving, Illustrating the South American Indians (1505)." *Bulletin of the New York Public Library* 34 (September): 755-60.

Eco, Umberto. 1979. *A Theory of Semiotics.* Advances in Semiotics. Bloomington, IN: Indiana University Press. Orig. ed. Indiana University Press.

_____. 1984. *Semiotics and the Philosophy of Language.* Advances in Semiotics. Bloomington, IN: Indiana University Press.

Eliade, Mircea. 1963. *Patterns in Comparative Religion.* Translation of *Traité d'histoire des Religions.* Orig. ed. Paris: Éditions Payot. Trans. Rosemary Sheed. New York: World Publishing Company, Meridian.

_____, ed. 1986. *The Encyclopedia of Religion.* New York: Macmillan.

Elizondo, Virgilio. 1977. "Our Lady of Guadalupe as a Cultural Symbol." In *Liturgy and Cultural Traditions.* Concilium. New York: Seabury Press, 25-33.

_____. 1978a. *The Human Quest: A Search for Meaning Through Life and Death.* Huntington, IN: Our Sunday Visitor, Inc.

_____. 1978b. *Mestizaje: The Dialectic of Cultural Birth and the Gospel.* San Antonio: Mexican American Cultural Center.

_____. 1983. *Galilean Journey: The Mexican-American Promise.* Maryknoll, NY: Orbis Books.

_____. 1988. *The Future is Mestizo: Life Where Cultures Meet.* Bloomington, IN: Meyer-Stone Books.

Elliot, J. H. 1963. *Imperial Spain: 1469-1650.* New York: Meridian Books.

_____. 1970. *The Old World and the New: 1492-1650.* Cambridge: Cambridge University Press.

_____. 1972. "The Discovery of America and the Discovery of Man." *Proceedings of the British Academy* 68: 101-25.

_____. 1989. *Spain and Its World: 1500-1700*. New Haven, CT: Yale University Press.

Evans, G. R. 1993. *Philosophy and Theology in the Middle Ages*. London: Routledge.

Fernández-Santamaria, J. A. 1977. *The State, War, and Peace: Spanish Political Thought in the Renaissance, 1516-1559*. Cambridge Studies in Early Modern History. Cambridge: Cambridge University Press.

Fuentes, Carlos. 1992. *The Buried Mirror: Reflections on Spain and the New World*. New York: Houghton Mifflin Co.

Funkestein, Amos. 1986. *Theology and the Scientific Imagination: From the Middle Ages to the Seventeenth Century*. Princeton, NJ: Princeton University Press.

Galeano, Eduardo. 1973. *Open Veins of Latin America: Five Centuries of the Pillage of a Continent*. New York: Monthly Review Press.

Galilea, Segundo. 1976. *Religiosidad Popular y Pastoral*. Madrid: Ediciones Cristiandad.

García-Rivera, Alejandro. 1993. "Artificial Intelligence and de las Casas: A 1492 Resonance." *Zygon* 28, no. 4 (December): 543-50.

_____. 1994a "A Contribution to the Dialogue between Theology and the Natural Sciences." *Journal of Hispanic/Latino Theology* 2, No. 1 (August): 51-59.

_____. 1994b. "Sacraments: Enter the World of God's Imagination." *U. S. Catholic* 59, No. 1 (January): 6-12.

Geertz, Clifford. 1973. *The Interpretation of Cultures: Selected Essays*. New York: Basic.

Genovese, Eugene. 1976. *Roll, Jordan, Roll: The World the Slaves Made*. New York: Random House, Inc.

Gerbi, Antonello. 1973. *The Dispute of the New World: The History of a Polemic, 1750-1900*. Translation of *La disputa del Nuovo Mondo: Storia di una polemica, 1750-1900*. Orig. ed. Italy: 1955. Trans. and rev. Jeremy Moyle. Pittsburgh: University of Pittsburgh Press.

_____. 1985. *Nature in the New World: From Christopher Columbus to Gonzalo Fernández de Oviedo*. Translation of *La natura delle Indie Nove: Da Cristofo Colombo a Gonzalo Fernández de Oviedo*. Orig. ed. Milan: Riccardo Ricciardi Editore, 1975. Trans. Jeremy Moyle. Pittsburgh: University of Pittsburgh Press.

Gilson, Etienne. 1940. *The Spirit of Medieval Philosophy.* Trans. A. H. C. Downes. New York: Scribner's.

_____. 1965. *The Philosophy of St. Bonaventure.* Paterson, NJ: St. Anthony Guild Press.

Gimenez, Gilberto. 1978. *Cultura Popular y Religion en el Anahuac.* México, D.F.: Centro de Estudios Ecuménicos.

Glacken, Clarence J. 1967. *Traces on the Rhodian Shore: Nature and Culture in Western Thought from Ancient Times to the End of the Eighteenth Century.* Berkeley, CA: University of California Press.

González, Justo L. 1990. *Mañana: Christian Theology from a Hispanic Perspective.* Nashville, TN: Abingdon Press.

Goodpasture, H. McKennie, ed. 1989. *Cross and Sword: An Eyewitness History of Christianity in Latin America.* Maryknoll, NY: Orbis Books.

Gramsci, Antonio. 1971. *Selections from the Prison Notebooks.* New York: International Publishers.

Green, Otis H. 1940. "A Note on Spanish Humanism. Sepúlveda and His Translation of Aristotle's Politics." *Hispanic Review* 8: 86-99.

Guerrero, Andrés. 1987. *A Chicano Theology.* Maryknoll, NY: Orbis Books.

Gutiérrez, Gustavo. 1977. *Teología desde el Reverso de la Historia.* Lima: DEI.

_____. 1990. *Teología de la Liberación.* With a new introduction, "Mirar Lejos." 7th ed. Lima: Centro de Estudios y Publicaciones. Orig. ed. 1968.

Haight, Roger, S.J. 1979. *The Experience and Language of Grace.* New York: Paulist Press.

Hamilton, Earl J. 1934. *American Treasure and the Price Revolution in Spain, 1501-1650.* Cambridge, MA: Harvard University Press.

Hanke, Lewis. 1959. *Aristotle and the American Indians: A Study in Race Prejudice in the Modern World.* Bloomington, IN: Indiana University Press.

Harris, Marvin. 1968. *The Rise of Anthropological Theory: A History of Theories of Culture.* New York: Thomas Y. Cromwell Company.

_____. 1980. *Cultural Materialism.* New York: Random House, Vintage.

_____. 1985. *Culture, People, Nature : An Introduction to General Anthropology.* Philadelphia: Harper & Row Publishers.

Harrison, Regina. 1989. *Signs, Songs, and Memory in the Andes: Translating Quechua Language and Culture.* Austin, TX: University of Texas Press.

Hartog, Francois. 1988. *The Mirror of Herodotus: The Representation of the Other in the Writing of History.* Trans. Janet Lloyd. Berkeley, CA: University of California Press.

Haslip-Viera, Gabriel. 1986. "The Underclass." In *Cities & Society in Colonial Latin America.* Ed. Louisa Schell Hoberman and Susan Midgen Socolow. Albuquerque, NM: University of New Mexico Press, 285-312..

Hefner, Philip. 1993. *The Human Factor.* Minneapolis, MN: Fortress Press.

Heiberg, J. L. 1920. "Théories Antiques sur l'Influence Moral du Climat." *Scientia* 27: 453-64.

Hoberman, Louisa Schell, and Susan Midgen Socolow, eds. 1986. *Cities & Society in Colonial Latin America.* Albuquerque, NM: University of New Mexico Press.

Hodge, Robert, and Gunther Kress. 1988. *Social Semiotics.* Ithaca, NY: Cornell University Press.

Hodgen, Margaret T. 1964. *Early Anthropology in the Sixteenth and Seventeenth Centuries.* Philadelphia: University of Pennsylvania Press.

Isambert, François-André. 1982. *Le Sens du Sacré: Fête et Religion Populaire.* Paris: Les Éditions de Minuit.

Isidore of Seville. 1911. *Scriptorum Classicorum Bibliotheca Oxoniensis.* Ed. W. M. Lindsay. 2 vols. *Etymologiarum Sive Originum.* Oxford: Oxford University Press.

Jones, W. R. 1971. "The Image of the Barbarian in Medieval Europe." *Comparative Studies in Society and History* 13 (October): 376-407.

Kearney, R. 1988. *The Wake of Imagination: Toward a Postmodern Culture.* Minneapolis, MN: University of Minnesota Press.

Keen, Benjamin. 1990. *The Aztec Image in Western Thought.* New Brunswick, NJ: Rutgers University Press.

_____, ed. 1986. *Latin American Civilization: History and Society, 1492 to Present.* Boulder, CO: Westview Press.

Kelsey, David H. 1982. "Human Being." In *Christian Theology: An Introduction to Its Tradition and Tasks.* Philadelphia: Fortress Press, 141-67.

Kemp, Eric Waldram. 1948. *Canonization and Authority in the Western Church.* Oxford: Oxford University Press.

Kiple, Kenneth F. 1987. "A Survey of Recent Literature on the Biological Past of Black People." In *The African Exchange: Toward a Biological History of Black People.* Ed. Kenneth F. Kiple. Durham, NC: Duke University Press, 7-34.

Klein, Herbert S. 1967. *Slavery in the Americas: A Comparative Study of Virginia and Cuba.* Chicago: University of Chicago Press.

_____. 1986. *African Slavery in Latin America and the Caribbean.* Oxford: Oxford University Press.

Kretzmann, Norman, Anthony Kenny, and Jan Pinborg, eds. 1982. *The Cambridge History of Later Medieval Philosophy.* Cambridge: Cambridge University Press.

Kroeber, A. L., and Clyde Kluckhohn. 1952. *Culture: A Critical Review of Concepts and Definitions.* Harvard University Peabody Museum of American Archaeology and Ethnology. Cambridge: Peabody Museum.

Lakoff, George, and Mark Turner. 1989. *More Than Cool Reason: A Field Guide to Poetic Metaphor.* Chicago: University of Chicago Press.

Langness, Lewis L. 1987. *The Study of Culture.* Rev. ed. Novato, CA: Chandler & Sharp Publishers, Inc.

Leclercq, Jean. 1987. "Influence and Noninfluence of Dionysius in the Western Middle Ages." In *Pseudo-Dionysius: The Complete Works.* Ed. John Farina. Classics of Western Spirituality. New York: Paulist Press, 25-32.

León-Portilla, Miguel, ed. 1963. *The Broken Spears: The Aztec Account of the Conquest.* Boston: Beacon Press.

Lévi-Strauss, Claude. 1966. *The Savage Mind.* Chicago: University of Chicago Press.

Lloyd, G. E. R. 1983. *Science, Folklore, and Ideology: Studies in the Life Sciences in Ancient Greece.* Cambridge: Cambridge University Press.

Lockhart, James. 1968. *Spanish Peru: 1532-1560: A Colonial Society.* Madison, WI: University of Wisconsin Press.

Lohmeyer, Ernst. 1936. *Galiläa und Jerusalem.* Göttingen: Vandenhoeck and Ruprecht.

López, Enrique Alvarez. 1940. "Plinio y Fernández de Oviedo." *Anales de Ciencias Naturales del Instituto J. de Acosta* 1: 46-61.

Lopez, Licenciado Greza, commentary by. 1974. *Las Siete Partidas del Sabio Rey Don Alonso el Nono.* Orig. ed. 1555. Madrid.

Lotman, M. Yuri. 1975. "On the Metalanguage of a Typological Description of Culture." *Semiotica* 14, No. 2: 97-123.

_____. 1990. *Universe of Mind: A Semiotic Theory of Culture.* With an introduction by Umberto Eco. Trans. Ann Shukman. Bloomington, IN: Indiana University Press.

Lovejoy, Arthur O. 1960. *The Great Chain of Being: A Study of the History of an Idea.* New York: Harper and Row, Harper Torchbooks/ Academy Library.

Lurker, Manfred. 1986. "Dogs." Trans. Matthew J. O'Connell. In *The Encyclopedia of Religion.* Ed. Mircea Eliade. Vol. 4. New York: Macmillan, 395-7.

Lyons, John. 1977. *Semantics.* Cambridge: Cambridge University Press.

Lyotard, Jean-François. 1988. *The Differend: Phrases in Dispute. Theory and History of Literature.* Minneapolis, MN: University of Minnesota Press.

McBride, Harry. 1968. *Vida Breve de Fray Martín de Porres.* Lima: Editorial Salesiana.

McDermott, Timothy, ed. 1989. *Summa Theologiae: A Concise Translation.* By Thomas Aquinas. Westminster, MD: Christian Classics.

McDonald, William J., ed. 1967a. *New Catholic Encyclopedia.* New York: McGraw Hill Co. s.v. "Canonization of Saints (History and Procedure)."

_____. 1967b. *New Catholic Encyclopedia.* New York: McGraw Hill Co. s.v. M. S. Nolde. "Emblem Books."

McGrane, Bernard. 1989. *Beyond Anthropology: Society and the Other.* New York: Columbia University Press.

Macken, Thomas F. 1909. *The Canonisation of Saints.* New York: Benziger Brothers.

McNeill, William H. 1976. *Plagues and People.* Garden City, NY: Anchor Press.

Mair, John (Johannes Major). 1519. *Secundum Librum Sententiarum.* Paris.

Maldonado, Luis. 1975. *Religiosidad Popular: Nostalgia de Lo Magico.* Mexico, DF: Ediciones Cristiandad.

_____. 1986. *Popular Religion: Its Dimensions, Levels and Types .* In *Popular Religion.* Ed. Norbert Greinacher and Norbert Mette. Edinburgh: T & T Clark, Ltd, 3-12.

Martin, Gerald. 1989. *Journeys Through the Labyrinth: Latin American Fiction in the Twentieth Century.* London: Verso.

Melendez, Juan, O.P. 1682.*Tesoros Verdaderos de las Indias en la Historia de la Gran Provincia de San Juan Bautista del Peru de el Orden Predicadores.* Vol. 3. 201-346. Rome: F. Ivan Melendez, 201-346. Orig. ed. 1673.

Michelet, Jules. 1855. *Histoire de France.* Vol. 7. Paris: University of Paris.

Mörner, Magnus. 1967. *Race Mixture in the History of Latin America.* Boston: Little, Brown and Company.

Niebuhr, H. Richard. 1956. *Christ and Culture.* New York: Harper and Row, Harper Torchbooks/ Cloister Library.

Nöth, Winfried. 1990. *Handbook of Semiotics.* Advances in Semiotics. Bloomington and Indianapolis, IN: Indiana University Press.

O'Callaghan, Joseph E. 1975. *A History of Medieval Spain.* Ithaca, NY: Cornell University Press.

Origen. 1969. *Contre Celse.* In *Sources Chrétiennes,* 1967-1976. Vol. 150. French and Greek. Introduction, critical text, ntrans. and notes by Marcel Borret. Paris: Editions du Cerf.

Pacchioni, Neri Romero de. N.d. *La Fascinante Vida del Santo Martín de Porres.* Lima: Centro de Proyección Cristiana.

Pacheco, Joaquín F., Francisco de Cárdenas, and Luis Torres de Mendoza, eds. 1864-84. *Colección de Documentos Inéditos Relativos al Descubrimiento, Conquista y Organización de las Antiguas Posesiones Españolas de América y Oceanía, Sacados de los Archivos del Reino y muy Especialmente de las Indias.* Madrid: N.p.

Padgen, Anthony. 1981. "The 'School of Salamanca' and the 'Affair of the Indies.'" In *History of Universities.* Vol. 1. *Continuity and Change in Early Modern Universities.* Avebury, 71-112.

_____. 1986. *The Fall of Natural Man: The American Indian and the Origin of Comparative Ethnology.* Cambridge Iberian and Latin American Studies. Cambridge: Cambridge University Press. Orig. ed. 1982.

Pandian, Jacob. 1991. *Culture, Religion, and the Sacred Self: A Critical Introduction to the Anthropological Study of Religion.* Englewood Cliffs, NJ: Prentice-Hall.

Parry, John H., and Robert G. Keith, eds. 1984. *New Iberian World: A Documentary History of the Discovery and Settlement of Latin America to the Early 17th Century.* 5 vols. New York: Times Books.

Patterson, Orlando. 1982. *Slavery and Social Death: A Comparative Study.* Cambridge, MA: Harvard University Press.

Penrose, Roger. 1989. *The Emperor's New Mind: Concerning Computers, Mind, and the Laws of Physics.* Foreword by Martin Gardner. Oxford: Oxford University Press.

Pereira, Juan de Solórzano. 1930. *Política Indiana.* Vol. 1. Madrid: N.p.

Perkins, George, Barbara Perkins, and Phillip Leininger, eds. 1991. "Magical Realism." In *Benét's Reader's Encyclopedia of American Literature.* New York: Harper Collins Publishers.

Pike, Kenneth L. 1967. *Language in Relation to a Unified Theory of the Structure of Human Behavior.* 2d ed. The Hague: Mouton. Orig. ed. 1954.

Preher, Sr. Leo Marie, O.P. 1941. *The Social Implications in the Work of Blessed Martin de Porres.* Ph. D. Diss. The Catholic University of America. Studies in Sociology. Vol. 4. Washington, DC: The Catholic University of America Press.

Prescott, William H. N.d. *History of the Conquest of Mexico and History of the Conquest of Peru.* New York: Random House, Inc.

Preus, J. Samuel. 1987. *Explaining Religion: Criticism and Theory from Bodin to Freud.* New Haven, CT, and London: Yale University Press.

Proceso de Beatificación de Fray Martín de Porres. See Secretariado Martín de Porres.

Procurator General of the Order of Friars Preachers. 1672. *Responsio Ad Novas Animadversiones R.P.D. Fidei Promotoris Super Dubio an Constet de Virtutibus Ecc. MS 15.* Vol. 3. Archives of the Postulation O.P. Rome

Pseudo-Dionysius. 1987. "The Ecclesiastical Hierarchy." In *Pseudo-Dionysius: The Complete Works.* Ed. John Farina. New York: Paulist Press.

Raboteau, Albert J. 1978. *Slave Religion: The "Invisible Institution" in the Antebellum South.* Oxford: Oxford University Press.

Rahner, Karl. 1933. "La Doctrine des 'Sens Spirituels' au Moyen-Age." *Revue d'Ascétique et de Mystique* 14, No. 55: 263-99.

_____. 1978. *Foundations of Christian Faith: An Introduction to the Idea of Christianity.* Translation of *Grundkurs des Glaubens: Einführung in den Begriff des Christentums.* Orig. ed. 1976. Trans. William V. Dych. New York: Seabury Press, Crossroads.

_____. 1981. "The Hiddenness of Being." In *A Rahner Reader.* Ed. Gerald A. McCool. New York: The Crossroads Publishing Company, 23-45.

Ray, Benjamin C. 1976. *African Religions: Symbol, Ritual, and Community.* Prentice-Hall Studies in Religion. Englewood Cliffs, NJ: Prentice-Hall.

Ricard, Robert. 1966. *The Spiritual Conquest of Mexico.* Orig. ed. *Conquête Spirituelle de Mexique.* Published as Volume XX of *Travaux et Mémoires de L'institute D'Ethnologie* by the University of Paris. Trans. Lesley Bird Simpson. California Library Reprint. Berkeley, CA: University of California Press.

Richard, Pablo, ed. 1980. *Materiales para una Historia de la Teología en América Latina.* San Jose, Costa Rica: Editorial DEI.

Rivera-Pagán, Luis N. 1991. *Evangelización y violencia: la conquista de América.* San Juan: Editorial Cemi.

Rodriguez, Jose David, and Colleen Nelson. 1986. "The Virgin of Guadalupe." In *Currents in Theology and Mission* 13, No. 6: 368-9.

Rout, Leslie B. 1976. *The African Experience in Spanish America: 1502 to the Present Day.* Cambridge Latin American Studies. Vol. 23. Cambridge: Cambridge University Press.

Rowe, William, and Vivian Schelling. 1991. *Memory and Modernity: Popular Culture in Latin America.* Critical studies in Latin American Culture. London: Verso.

Ruffié, Jacques. 1983. *De la Biologie a la Culture.* New and Revised Edition. 2 vols. Champ Scientifique. Paris: Flammarion.

Scannone, Juan Carlos. 1984. *Sabiduria Popular, Símbolo y Filosofía: Dialogo Internacional en Torno a Una Interpretación Latino Americana.* Buenos Aires: Editorial Guadalupe.

Schreiter, Robert J. 1985. *Constructing Local Theologies.* Maryknoll, NY: Orbis Books.

Sebeok, Thomas A. 1991. *A Sign Is Just a Sign.* Bloomington, IN: Indiana University Press.

Secretariado Martín de Porres. 1960. Translation from the Latin Into Spanish of the Official Process of Beatification of St. Martin of Porres During the Years 1660-1674. In *Proceso de Beatificación de Fray Martín de Porres.* Palencia: Secretariado "Martin de Porres." Orig. ed. 1660-1671.

Segovia, Fernando F. 1991. "A New Manifest Destiny: The Emerging Theological Voice of Hispanic Americans." *Religious Studies Review* 17, No. 2: 101-9.

Sepúlveda, Juan Ginés. 1892. "Democrates Alter Sive de Justis Belli Causis Apud Indos." *Boletín de la Real Academia de la Historia* 21 (November): 260-381. Orig. ed. 1550.

Sheldon, Huntington. 1988. *Boyd's Introduction to the Study of Disease.* 10th ed. Philadelphia: Lea & Febiger.

Shweder, Richard A. 1991. *Thinking Through Cultures: Expeditions in Cultural Psychology.* Cambridge: Cambridge University Press.

Silverblatt, Irene. 1987. *Moon, Sun and Witches: Gender Ideologies and Class in Inca and Colonial Peru.* Princeton, NJ: Princeton University Press.

Siraisi, Nancy G. 1990. *Medieval & Early Renaissance Medicine: An Introduction to Knowledge and Practice.* Chicago: University of Chicago Press.

Smith, Adam. 1937. *An Inquiry into the Nature and Causes of the Wealth of Nations.* Ed. and notes Edwin Cannan. With an introduction by Edwin Cannan and Max Lerner. New York: Modern Library.

Smith, Jonathan Z. 1985. "What a Difference a Difference Makes." In *To See Ourselves as Others See Us: Christians, Jews, "Others" in Late Antiquity.* Ed. Jacob Neusner and Ernest S. Frerichs. Studies in the Humanities. Chico, CA: Scholars Press, 3-48.

Soler, Luis M. Diaz. 1953. *Historia de la Esclavitud Negra en Puerto Rico.* San Juan: Editorial Universitaria de la Universidad de Puerto Rico.

Souvay, Charles L. 1907. "Animals in the Bible." In *The Catholic Encyclopedia.* Ed. Charles G. Herbermann. Vol. 1. New York: Robert Appleton Company, 517-26.

Stern, Steve J. 1982. *Peru's Indian Peoples and the Challenge of Spanish Conquest: Huamanga to 1640.* Madison, WI: University of Wisconsin Press.

Sullivan, Lawrence. 1986. "Healing." In *The Encyclopedia of Religion.* Ed. Mircea Eliade. Vol. 6. New York: Macmillan, 226-34.

_____. 1988. *Icanchu's Drum: An Orientation to Meaning in South American Religions.* Chicago: University of Chicago Press.

Theunissen, Michael. 1984. *The Other: Studies in the Social Ontology of Husserl, Heidegger, Sartre, and Buber.* Cambridge, MA: MIT Press.

Thils, G. 1977. "La 'Religion Populaire': Approches, Définition." *Revue Théologique de Louvain* 8: 198-210.

Thurston, Herbert, S.J. 1952. "The Odour of Sanctity." In *The Physical Phenomena of Mysticism.* Chicago: Henry Regnery Company, 222-32.

Tillich, Paul. 1932. *The Religious Situation.* Trans. H. Richard Niebuhr. New York: Henry Holt Co.

_____. 1951. *Systematic Theology.* Vol. 1. Chicago: University of Chicago Press.

_____. 1987. *On Art and Architecture*. New York: Crossroads Publishing Company.

Todorov, Tzvetan. 1982. *Theories of the Symbol*. Translation of *Théories du symbole*. Orig. ed. 1977. Trans. Catherine Porter. Ithaca, NY: Cornell University Press.

_____. 1984. *The Conquest of America*. Trans. Richard Howard. New York: Harper & Row Publishers.

Towler, Robert. 1975. *Homo Religiosus: Sociological Problems in the Study of Religion*. New York: St. Martin's Press.

Tracy, David. 1981. *The Analogical Imagination: Christian Theology and the Culture of Pluralism*. New York: Crossroads.

_____. 1989. "The Uneasy Alliance Reconceived: Catholic Theological Method, Modernity, and Postmodernity." *Theological Studies* 50: 548-70.

Turner, Victor. 1974. *Dramas, Fields, and Metaphors: Symbolic Action in Human Society. Symbol, Myth, and Ritual*. Ithaca, NY: Cornell University Press.

Uexkhüll, Jakob von. 1973. *Theoretische Biologie*. Frankfurt: Suhrkamp. Orig. ed. 1928.

Valtierra, Angel, S.J. 1960. *Peter Claver: Saint of the Slaves*. Translation of *El Santo Que Liberto Una Raza San Pedro Claver, S.J.* Bogotá, 1954. With a preface by James Brodick, S.J. Trans. Janet H. Perry and L. J. Woodward. Westminster: Newman Press.

van den Broek, R. 1979. "Popular Religious Practices and Ecclesiastical Policies in the Early Church." In *Official and Popular Religion: Analysis of a Theme for Religious Studies*. Ed. Pieter Vrijhof and Jacques Waardenburg. Paris: Mouton & Co., 11-54.

Vasconcelos, José. N.d. *La Raza Cósmica*. Mexico City, DF: Agencia Mundial de Librería.

Vrijhof, Pieter Hendrik. 1979. "Introduction." In *Official and Popular Religion: Analysis of a Theme for Religious Studies*. Ed. Jacques Waardenburg and Pieter Hendrik Vrijhof. New York: Mouton Publishers, 1-10.

Walbank, F. W. 1957. *A Historical Commentary on Polybius*. 3 vols. Oxford: Oxford University Press.

Walens, Stanley. 1986. "Animals." In *The Encyclopedia of Religion*. Ed. Mircea Eliade. Vol. 1. New York: Macmillan, 291-6.

Warnock, Mary. 1978. *Imagination*. Berkeley, CA: University of California Press.

Weatherford, Jack. 1988. *Indian Givers: How the Indians of the Americas Transformed the World.* New York: Ballantine Books.

Weinstein, Donald, and Rudolph M. Bell. 1982. *Saints & Society: The Two Worlds of Western Christendom, 1000-1700.* Chicago: The University of Chicago Press.

Winner, Irene Portis, and Thomas G. Winner. 1976. "The Semiotics of Cultural Texts." *Semiotica* 18, No. 2: 101-56.

Zavala, Silvio A. 1971. *Las Instituciones Jurídicas en la Conquista de América.* Rev. and enlarged ed. Mexico City: Editorial Porrúa.

Zerries, Otto. 1986. "Lord of the Animals." In *The Encyclopedia of Religion.* Ed. Mircea Eliade. Vol. 9. New York: Macmillan, 22-5.

Index

INDEX